DATE DUE

Additional Praise for

SELLING LUXURY

"Today, our customers' references in terms of service are extremely high and go far beyond the luxury sector. In the world of luxury, customers are expecting a top level of service before, during, and after every contact or sale. Reaching excellence in service is essential for each Sales Ambassador so that customers are even more satisfied and loyal to the brand. This everyday challenge should be approached humbly, with the understanding that it is a never-ending learning process."

—Bernard Fornas, CEO, Cartier International

SELLING
LUXURY

Connect with Affluent Customers,
Create Unique Experiences Through
Impeccable Service, and Close the Sale

ROBIN LENT
and
GENEVIÈVE TOUR

WILEY

John Wiley & Sons, Inc.

To Sales Ambassadors
all over the world

Contents

Foreword by Alain-Dominique Perrin   *xi*

Acknowledgments   *xiii*

Introduction   *xv*

Part One: Initial Thoughts   *1*

1	The Vital Role of the Sales Ambassador	3
2	In the eyes of the customer, the Sales Ambassador is the brand	5
3	Loyalty begins with the first contact	6
4	Keep in mind how you like to be treated	7
5	There are customers behind customers	8
6	The incredible loss from one lost customer	9
7	The emotional side of the purchase	10
8	The island vacation or the earrings?	11
9	The price is only one of the factors	12
10	The "Wow" comes when you go beyond expectations	13
11	Discretion and confidentiality	14

Part Two: The Frame of Mind of the Sales Ambassador   *17*

12	Be a person before being a Sales Ambassador	19
13	Turn every contact into an experience	20
14	Get inside the customer's story	21
15	Congratulate customers	23
16	Compliment your customers	24
17	Every complaint is an opportunity	25
18	The other competitor	26
19	Service costs nothing	28
20	The great danger of prejudices and preconceived ideas	29
21	Work as a team player	30
22	Relationships and mistakes	31

Part Three: The Savoir-Faire of the Sales Ambassador 35

23	The successful selling style	37
24	Life is a celebration	38
25	Use each contact to inform and educate	39
26	The power of timing	40
27	Time is a precious sales tool	42
28	The art of using silence	44
29	Music as a metaphor for selling	45
30	Select the words you use carefully	46
31	Tones, rhythms, and volumes	47
32	The competition, your customers, and your advantages	48
33	Personalize your service	49
34	Pleasure comes from consistency	50
35	Maintain your energy	51
36	Make someone's day	53
37	Each telephone contact is another opportunity	54
38	Analyze the sale you made	56
39	Analyze the situation when the customer did not buy	58

Part Four: Preparing to Sell 61

40	The impact of the right atmosphere on customers	63
41	Luxury is in the details	65
42	Keep the service level up even when things are busy	66
43	Prepare your selling tools	68
44	Know what you have in stock	69
45	Learn how each creation was crafted	70
46	Know what is happening in your city	71

Part Five: Welcoming and Discovering the Customer 73

47 A greeting needs a smile   75
48 Your body language speaks louder than words   76
49 Listening with your eyes   77
50 The importance of discovery   79
51 The gift purchase   81
52 The power of questions (quality over quantity)   82
53 Be a careful listener   84
54 Find out how your customer feels about your brand   85
55 Make statements to obtain information   86
56 Introduce yourself   87
57 "Just looking"   88
58 The art and importance of reformulation   90

Part Six: Proposing, Romancing, and Handling Objections 93

59 Keep your proposals simple   95
60 Create curiosity   96
61 Handle everything you sell as a precious object   98
62 Position the offer   100
63 Make clever use of the light   102
64 Romance your creations to enhance the emotions   103
65 Storytelling   104
66 Invite the customer to try on the model   106
67 "Wrap" the price as if it were a gift   108
68 The art of exploring "Let me think about it"   109
69 Prepare for dealing with objections   111

Part Seven: Concluding and Making Additional Sales   113

70	Be aware of buying signals	115
71	Tips to conclude	117
72	Suggest the best solution	119
73	The importance of reassuring when concluding	120
74	"Picture" the purchase	122
75	Advise customers about maintaining their purchase	123
76	Suggest ways of offering a gift	125
77	The additional sale	126

Part Eight: Building Customer Loyalty   129

78	Loyalty comes from offering gifts linked to the purchase	131
79	Offer two business cards	132
80	Make a good last impression	133
81	Every departure is a preparation for another visit	134
82	Loyalty comes from remembering your customers	136
83	The database is an essential tool	137
84	Celebrate the newborn	138
85	Build loyalty by staying in touch	140
86	Ask for a referral	142
87	Customer after-sales service and the broken dream	144
88	The ideal after-sales service scenario	146

Outcomes of the Eight Stories   149

Conclusion   153

Index   156

Foreword

Selling in a luxury universe is full of magic, passion, and emotion. The customer, the creation, and the Sales Ambassador all enjoy an exchange of views that is just as important as the object itself and its beauty. In this way, the Sales Ambassador builds a relationship and actively participates in the brand experience.

The role of the Sales Ambassador is vital for the success and future of every brand. Selling is a noble profession that is both complex and diverse. It requires a multitude of skills, personal energy, and the ability to be constantly self-motivated.

Brand managers value their Sales Teams, recognizing their achievements and the importance of their role in growing the business. It is my experience that Sales Ambassadors also become excellent sources of information through their contacts with customers. Because of this, Sales Ambassadors can also be involved in suggesting new creations and models.

Selling Luxury is a gem, unique in the world of luxury. Geneviéve Tour and Robin Lent have brought together their contacts and personal experiences to create a book that is full of excellent advice and practical examples on both understanding the art of luxury selling and keeping customer loyalty.

Successful Sales Ambassadors are always on the lookout for ways to improve the quality of their contacts. Even for the best of them, this book will add to their "savoir-faire," sharpen their skills, and increase their pleasure as they participate in building the brand experience.

Selling Luxury presents selling as the rich and fascinating world it is when approached with passion and professionalism.

—Alain-Dominique Perrin
Executive Director, Companie Financière Richemont,
and President, Ecole des Dirigeants et
Créateurs d'entreprise (EDC), Paris

Acknowledgments

We are very grateful to our agent, Bob Silverstein of Quicksilver Books, for his trust and belief in this book.

Sincere thanks as well to our editor, Richard Narramore, for his support and insight and to his assistant, Ann Kenny, for guiding us through the editorial process.

We are also grateful to Charlotte Duntze and François Le Troquer for giving us access to their networks and many contacts.

Sincere thanks to Caroline Lent and Allan Sanders, our proofreaders, for their advice, corrections, and many helpful suggestions.

Introduction

What happens in a luxury environment that makes it unique? How do you build customer loyalty that can last for decades or even a lifetime? What is the link between a luxury creation and the person dreaming of owning it? How can you give added value compared to the competition? How do you go about up-selling or cross-selling in a luxury environment? How can you take advantage of customer after-sales service situations? How can approaches such as using silence and observation play an active role in the sales process? What are customers really shopping for when they visit a luxury boutique?

Selling Luxury answers these questions and many more using our combined 30 years of personal experience in selling and training in luxury as well as our contacts with top Sales Ambassadors throughout the world. These "tips from the best" offer pertinent keys to luxury selling.

These 88 approaches are given in a clear and practical manner and are ready to use immediately. At first, some of the points, such as the importance of greeting, smiling, and listening may seem to be nonspecific for the luxury universe. We can assure you that based on our research these basics are essential and very much expected from customers shopping in a luxury universe.

The importance of the role of Sales Ambassadors cannot be stated often enough. They *are* the brand for the customer. Each Sales Ambassador is responsible for creating the experience that customers will always remember. For those working in sales, applying *Selling Luxury* is an excellent way to improve performance.

How do you define a luxury customer? It is very simple. We are all luxury customers. We all have our own personal luxury. It could be the park bench we like to sit on and read the paper, the place we go to on Saturday mornings for coffee, or the spot where we go to watch the sunset. We all have those little unique and special things that matter to us, a little luxury that makes us feel special.

What about shopping? Are only the rich and superrich considered luxury customers? Absolutely not. People decide that they want something unique, either for someone they love or for themselves. Their incomes may be very modest. The cost of a creation is far less important than the desire to mark the event or special occasion between family and friends, whether it is a birth, an anniversary, a graduation, or a promotion. Life is a celebration, and to have something exceptional to remember those special moments adds to the pleasure.

Luxury has been with us since the pharaohs in Egypt some 6,000 years ago and probably even much earlier. Luxury will continue to be here in one form or another in the future. Brands may disappear, but the notion of luxury is a part of us and will stay with us.

In *Selling Luxury*, we have differentiated the Sales Ambassador from the Sales Associate in order to give clear examples in each situation about what should be done and what should be avoided. We have also alternated between "he" and "she" throughout the book, either to identify the Sales Ambassador or the customer. We have purposely not used brand names in our examples for two reasons. First of all, we wanted the brands to remain confidential. There is a discretion in luxury that we have respected. The second reason was to avoid having readers think that certain approaches were only valid in specific fields of luxury sales. We have found that *Selling Luxury* performs well across a variety of sales situations. Why 88 points? There are several reasons for our choice. In the same way that, during a sale, there is a symbolism or story behind each creation, there is also a symbolism behind "the eights":

◆ Eight is the symbol of balance and harmony, which is a constant challenge in building relationships between Sales Ambassadors and customers.

◆ Eight, in mathematics, is the symbol of infinity. Here we thought of the notion of having lasting relationships with customers.

◆ In numerology, 8 is the symbol of someone who has mastered knowledge. *Selling Luxury* will certainly improve the skills and competencies of Sales Ambassadors wishing to be virtuosos in the field of luxury.

◆ Finally, in certain cultures, Chinese for instance, the number 8 symbolizes good luck and happiness. In Cantonese, the number eight is pronounced "fa." This is the same pronunciation as the sound for "to grow richer" in the large sense of the word. Two eights double the possibilities.

May Selling Luxury be an enrichment for those who read it!

At the end of each chapter, you will find a story that gives a real-life customer and Sales Ambassador situation. Each story ends with a question for the reader to imagine the outcomes (impact and result). The outcomes of each of the eight examples are listed together at the end of the book.

Luxury means paying tribute to customers seeking perfection from creations while being waited on by exceptional salespersons. Selling and service are at the forefront of every luxury brand. Selling is a professional art, and only excellence is acceptable from luxury sales staff. If you are seeking enjoyment and fulfillment, you should consider becoming a salesperson in the world of luxury.

—*Michel Guten*
President, Institut Supérieur de Marketing du Luxe;
Vice-President Délégué du Comité des Champs-Elysées;
Former CEO, Lancel;
Former Vice-Président, Cartier France

The *Vital Role*

1 of the Sales Ambassador

The publicity photograph in the magazine shows a stunning, sensual, young woman with a top brand-name handbag on her shoulder. The handbag is chic and beautifully designed. While traveling into town, the potential buyer observes this image and makes a mental note of the name of the impressive creation.

She takes time during her lunch break to go to the boutique located in an area where there are many other luxury brands. There, in the window, is the same handbag, looking even more appealing than in the advertisement.

The potential buyer does what many of us do when we see something we want. She starts to justify why she should have it. She finds at least half a dozen good reasons why she absolutely needs, deserves, has to have that handbag.

She walks to the door to enter the boutique.

The next few minutes are crucial to the brand. The company has spent time and money with marketing, designers, craftsmen, and a variety of experts to choose the materials and make the creation, not to mention logistics, packaging, quality approval, testing, and the list goes on.

Now it is the Sales Ambassador's turn. If he fails, everything that has been done before has no meaning or purpose.

Through the glass door the Sales Ambassador can see the woman entering. Just as important as seeing her is understanding that her expectations are extremely high. She has already begun to have a strong desire to own the beautiful piece. But when the contact is not at the right level, the bubble can be easily burst. If she sees the brand as overpromising and underdelivering, the magic fades.

The Sales Ambassador knows that it is essential to have a presence and approach that is elegant but friendly, one that will quickly put the woman at ease in the universe she is entering. With a welcoming smile on his face, he approaches as the doorman opens the door for the woman.

Customers expect service to be at the same level as the creations brands are promoting.

2
In the eyes of the customer, the Sales Ambassador *is the brand*

For each contact with a customer, it is important to remember that the Sales Ambassador *is* the brand for the customer. When your demeanor invokes positive feelings in the customer, the chances for completing a successful sale are increased. The better the customer feels about the entire process, the stronger the possibility of completing the sale will be. The term "Ambassador" is important here. The Sales Ambassador truly represents the brand.

When a contact is negative, the whole brand is seen as negative. Consider the Sales Associate who becomes exasperated or indifferent with a customer, who in turn then leaves angry and/or disappointed. The Sales Associate was the brand for the customer, a brand that has failed in her eyes.

Upstream, a great deal of energy and work has been put into bringing the creations to the customer. When bearing in mind just the designing, creating, marketing, and communication required up to this point, Sales Ambassadors understand how critical their role is in the whole process.

The Sales Ambassador's positive role is essential for the brand. If the creation does not sell, the whole process grinds to a halt.

Sales Ambassadors have a vital role to play in the brand's success.

Loyalty begins
with the first contact

3

Where does loyalty come from? From trusting someone. There can be no loyalty without trust. Trust is something that is built with each contact: "*I can trust this person a little more.*"

Therefore the opportunity of building trust with someone begins by putting that person at ease right from the first contact. Is this contact with the Sales Ambassador honest and sincere? How does the Sales Ambassador show that she really cares about the person? Could other helpful advice be shared?

Helping customers find what they want and providing solutions for their needs are both parts of building trust and loyalty.

There are fewer things more fragile than trust. Although it may develop little by little over a period of time, it can be shattered with one blow. One contradiction, one insincere comment, one dishonest, or even seemingly dishonest situation, can destroy in a moment a trust that has been meticulously built over time.

Sales Ambassadors know that loyalty is the key to long-term success. They make sure that trust remains something that is built over time, and that any possibility of trust being broken is eliminated.

Building trust is the best way to build loyalty.

4 Keep in mind how you like to *be treated*

It's almost too simple. It closely resembles the old Golden Rule: "Do unto others. . . ." Sales Ambassadors start with their own personal impressions. They evaluate the service they receive in situations all the time.

Here are some of the frequent responses that people give when asked the question *"Why are you loyal to certain places?"*

"They remember my name."
"The Sales staff is never pushy."
"I feel good when I enter."
"It is a positive experience. Even if I do not buy, people are glad to see me and help me."
"The staff is honest and sincere."
"The Sales Ambassador sent me a 'thank-you' note."

Customers will also reveal the way they like to be treated. We all have different preferences for how we want to be approached. Sales Ambassadors observe and analyze behaviors. For example: "Is this someone who likes to be left alone for a while or who would prefer more immediate assistance?" The ability to have a flexible and adaptive style is essential in building customer relationships with a variety of people.

The strength of a brand and the quality of its creations do of course play a role. But much more derives in large part from the quality and service given by the Sales Ambassador.

How do you like being treated?
Develop an adaptable approach.

5 There are customers *behind* customers

When people shop, they are often searching for something that goes beyond minimum expectations. They may want more than simply to go to a place displaying objects. When they shop, they want an experience.

Years ago, a hairdresser we know had a very good experience at a luxury jeweler's. A bracelet given to her by her grandmother needed repairing. While she was there, the Sales Ambassador let her try on a beautiful diamond ring. There was no attempt to sell it to her. It was just for fun, the pleasure of seeing it on her finger.

Eight years later, she still tells this story. For eight years she has sent hundreds of customers to the jeweler. Once the contact became an enjoyable experience, she became an Ambassador of the brand.

A strange story? Of course not. It happens every day, all over the world. It happens with every pleasant experience. People remember the pleasure. When you make customers' visits metamorphose into experiences, they, in turn, give you access to their network. They happily share their positive experiences with people they meet and know.

The Sales Ambassador understands that there is more to a successful sale than having the customer make a purchase. Each customer visit is seen in the long term, opening the door to other opportunities for the customer to return and share the experience with family, friends, and colleagues.

Develop your network fast through making each customer contact an experience.

The incredible *loss* from one *lost* customer

6

Losing a customer means more than losing one person. It also means losing access to their universe and the people they know. In other words, their network is no longer available to you.

A customer goes away dissatisfied because of a poor welcome and unacceptable service. If his children, parents, colleagues at work, friends, people he plays sports with, or even someone he meets at a conference somewhere needs something you could supply, he won't suggest going to see you.

But it is worse than just cutting you off from dozens of good contacts and potential customers. Unhappy lost customers, even the ones who do not complain directly to you before leaving, will spread negative information about the poor service they received.

When one customer leaves unhappy,
you lose dozens of contacts and opportunities.

The *emotional* side
7 of the purchase

When considering a person's buying habits, it is important to understand why certain creations, which obviously go beyond their functionality, are being purchased.

People don't buy a sports car to get from A to B, a luxury watch to know what time it is, or a beautiful hand-stitched travel bag because they have things to carry.

If they simply wanted to get from A to B, they would drive any car or take public transportation. If they just wanted to know what time it was, they could buy an inexpensive watch. If they only wanted to carry things, they could use a plastic bag.

They buy these objects because design and style have an uplifting impact on their lives. People feel the pleasure that comes from owning and being in contact with the quality and beauty of the creation.

Customers also want to make a statement about who they are and show their tastes. At times, they make purchases to be seen as belonging to a certain group. Other times, the reason can be distinctly the opposite, they want their purchase to set them apart from everyone else.

A Sales Ambassador's role is to understand that customer requests are more than the mere functionality of an item. A gentleman once purchased a necklace for the simple pleasure of having it on display in his living room as a work of art.

When the Sales Ambassador moves into the realm of dreams and emotions, the exchanges that take place in this universe are very different.

Go beyond functionality. Be a dream seller.

8

The *island vacation* or the *earrings?*

Sales Ambassadors understand that they are competing against a variety of choices, including the possibility that the person may not buy at all. Competition is everywhere. Take travel agencies and the possibilities of a vacation as an example.

A couple has been together for five years and they are now thinking very seriously about how to celebrate their upcoming wedding anniversary. They visit a travel agency to obtain information about taking an island vacation—two weeks off, lie in the sun, and just relax together. Because they both work, they could use the rest.

Early one evening, they are out walking and stop to look in a window of a well-known brand's boutique at a beautiful pair of earrings. The woman cannot hide how much she likes them. Her grandmother (whom she adored) had a similar pair.

The next day, the man decides to visit the boutique. He and his wife are hesitating on whether they should really take two weeks off. Maybe it would be a better idea for him to buy his wife those lovely earrings and then take her out to a nice restaurant. The price? Well, it's pretty much the same. As he walks into the boutique, in his mind he cannot help thinking "*The vacation or the earrings?*"

In the boutique, the salesperson does not take him seriously. She does little to welcome him and nothing to find out why he is interested in the earrings. The man soon has the impression that he is unwelcome. He is treated so poorly that he feels uncomfortable and leaves the boutique.

The following week, the couple flies off to their island vacation.

Remember, you could be competing with a travel agency.

The price is *only one*
of the factors

9

One of the key points that all Sales Ambassadors understand is that price is only one of the reasons people buy.

But forget Sales Ambassadors for a moment and ask yourself the question "Do I always go to the cheapest place to eat, buy the cheapest clothes, use places that offer the cheapest services?" The answer is, of course, no, you don't.

And why not? Because buying and selling is more complex than just what the price says. You go someplace because that "something else" is happening there. There is an energy; there are good quality offers in both creations and services.

This does not mean that price-oriented people will not come to shop at your place. But if they have only come to you for the price, then they will leave for the price, as soon as they find cheaper somewhere else.

Offer them the best service you can and avoid lowering the price. When you do give a lower price, you undervalue the quality, the savoir-faire, and the image of the brand.

Impeccable personalized service
justifies the price.

10

The *"Wow"* comes when you go beyond expectations

Along with being consistent, Sales Ambassadors look for ways to deliver a delightful and unexpected level of service. They are constantly finding ways to create an unforgettable experience with each customer. Often, it is the little things that make this happen.

Some examples:

✦ While visiting India, a Sales Ambassador brings back a special package of the customer's favorite tea.

✦ An after-sales service center that fills a rush order so that the customer can take the piece with her on a trip.

✦ The delivery of a gift that would normally not be available for an anniversary, but because of exceptional service, arrives just in time.

✦ A restaurant owner who offers without charge photographs of customers celebrating an event.

✦ A luxury hotel that prints complimentary business cards for their guests with their name and contact numbers at the hotel.

Everyday opportunities exist to create an unforgettable moment, so that customers share with others the incredible service they received.

"You won't believe what happened to me! I was in (the name of a boutique), and the Sales Ambassador . . ." followed by the story of their astonishing experience.

To create the "Wow," exceed expectations every time.

Discretion
11 and *confidentiality*

A customer who has established a person-to-person contact with a Sales Ambassador wants conversations and purchases to be kept confidential. The longer a Sales Ambassador knows a customer, the more the customer will share with him. This information, sometimes very personal, is given because trust has been established between both parties.

We mentioned earlier how fragile trust is. Discretion on the part of the Sales Ambassador is essential in maintaining the relationship. Along with personal information, purchases should also be kept confidential. Beyond the obvious security issue, in particular with high-priced creations, the question of who the purchase was made for could be very sensitive. A Sales Ambassador might be told one thing, whereas something else happens.

Customers dislike finding out that there were conversations about them behind their backs. They begin to doubt and wonder what was actually said. So when the opportunity to divulge something about Mr. X's purchase last week and how much his wife is going to like it comes up, the Sales Ambassador simply makes it perfectly clear that discretion is one of the rules of the house.

What else is the Sales Ambassador saying when she does not gossip about another customer? She is telling those doing the asking that she will also be discreet about them. Customers know that if there is talk and gossip about others, then they will be talked about as well.

Building long-term relationships requires discretion.

Story 1

A businessman had been coming to the luxury Japanese hotel for more than a decade. Every year he booked one of the prestigious rooms at two different times during the year, meaning that he stayed 30 days per year in the hotel and also used their spa facilities. The gentleman was well known by many of the staff who greeted him by his name. For a special occasion, the VIP customer booked a table for several of his closest friends for a dinner party. The evening was wonderfully run, the food delicious. But when the guests left after thanking their host, they were each billed for parking their car in the hotel's parking lot. One friend happened to mention this to the host a few days later. The VIP customer called the hotel to find out why they were billed, and happened to have someone on the telephone who did not recognize who he was. "Sir, we are only following policy and when people use our parking, they are charged for it!"

How do you think this concluded? See page 149.

Part Two: The Frame of Mind of the Sales Ambassador

Sales Ambassadors are first and foremost people. Education, experience, and culture are the basics, but the real gifts are personality and passion. Some are more successful than others because they go further. They embody their job and feel unique because they understand that their clients are unique. They feel lucky and want to bring luck to their clients. They have an immense pleasure in making their clients happy.

—François Le Troquer
General Manager, Cartier Russia and CIS

Be a person before being a Sales Ambassador

12

Selling is all about developing relationships, one at a time, one after the other. Throughout a selling day, as Sales Ambassadors meet customers for the first time, they find out about each person—who they are, what their tastes and interests are—going beyond the request to buy.

Even if someone has come in and has been very specific about what he wants to see, a Sales Ambassador still comes back to a personalized approach. They are, first of all, two human beings, sharing a moment together. So the Sales Ambassador finds out more about the person.

Far too often an error is made when a Sales Associate becomes too caught up in his or her role of being "the Seller," and immediately tags the people coming into the store as "the potential customer." First and foremost, you are a person.

Think of the places you go when you shop or seek services. Often, it is because the people who work there are sincerely interested in us, in who we are. They have connected with us as individuals. When we return, we feel pleasure in seeing each other again.

Establish person-to-person contact first, and then move into selling.

13

Turn every *contact* into an *experience*

Here is a goal for each Sales Ambassador: *"Make every contact a pleasurable experience, whether it is someone who is purchasing or not."* In other words, all people who leave the boutique and later think about their visit will remember being impressed by the way they were treated, regardless of whether they were a customer or a visitor.

The Sales Ambassadors know that for this to work, they need to personalize and make each contact unique and exceptional. A variety of appropriate approaches should be tailored to the situation, sometimes with humor, other times being informative, yet another helpful, or offering an unexpected but very appreciated service that was needed at that moment. Each person goes away positively surprised by what happened.

These little gestures of kindness matter. Sales Ambassadors often mention that they receive a lot of energy back when they practice giving, and that, because they are having fun at the same time, the time passes more quickly.

Making each contact's day might just make your day!

Get inside

14

the *customer's story*

We recently went to test a luxury brand's sales skills. Our scenario was that we were pretending to be a couple looking for wedding rings.

In one of their beautiful stores in London, a young, attractive saleswoman greeted us.

Man from the couple: *"We're looking for wedding rings."*
Saleswoman: *"Do you know your finger sizes?"*

We were shocked, speechless. There we were, planning one of the most important events of our lives, filled with emotion and passion, and the saleswoman wants to know our finger sizes! Her statement was enough to drive us both straight out the door and into one of the competitor's boutiques, which was just down the street. With this type of response, how many potential customers had she lost that day? That month?

A Sales Ambassador remembers the importance of establishing a personal relationship with the customer. She also remembers that there are plenty of good offers available from competitors and that most couples will shop around. This first contact should be a moment to find out more about the future couple's story. But first, *"Congratulations! How nice of you to choose (the brand name). We have some exceptional creations I'd love to show you. Tell me, when are you getting married?"*

From the answer to this question, the Sales Ambassador receives valuable information. She will know if the wedding has been planned and if the ring choice has been left to the last minute.

The Sales Ambassador can also ask:
"Where are you planning to get married?"

Again, it is a time for the Sales Ambassador to listen and observe. Is he (or she) still hesitating about taking the big jump?

The Sales Ambassador:
"Tell me more about what you have in mind?"

How classical or contemporary are they? What does this say about the designs the Sales Ambassador will propose?

Everyone comes in with a story that needs to be discovered.

15

Congratulate customers

"Congratulations" is a word that should be heard all day long. Many customers are purchasing for someone else or for a special occasion. Sincerely congratulating them values their decision to make a purchase for someone they love. It is always a pleasure to be recognized when making a gesture.

Congratulations can be given at the beginning but also when something is discovered. The Sales Ambassador discovers that the gentleman wants something for his daughter who has just graduated from university. A couple is looking for a wedding anniversary gift for her after seven years of marriage. A young man just got his first job and wants to purchase a gift for himself.

"Congratulations" is also a word that should always be used when the purchase is completed. Once the customer decides to buy, the first phrase out of the mouth of the Sales Ambassador should be *"Congratulations, you've made a wonderful choice."*

Congratulate, congratulate, congratulate (with sincerity)!

Compliment
your customers

16

Giving compliments is a great tool for many reasons. We wear or use certain items that we have chosen and that we like. A compliment is flattering to the customer, and who does not like to be sincerely flattered once in a while? It can also reassure someone about a purchase he has made.

Last but not least, it can be a way to start a conversation with your customer and create a pleasant atmosphere.

If you see a customer wearing two diamond rings and a pair of diamond earrings, the Sales Ambassador could say: *"You are wearing some exquisite diamond pieces that suit you so well!"*

From experience and discussions with top Sales Ambassadors, we know that they do not let a day go by without giving compliments.

Compliments can be about many different things: clothes, jewelry, health, hair, makeup, or personal events.

Giving compliments is a MUST.

17

Every *complaint* is an *opportunity*

Actually finding solutions for one customer's complaints can prove advantageous for other customers. Changing what was irritating or making one customer unhappy may prove to be an improvement for all of your customers.

A customer complained that the delay on sold-out models was too long. Looking into it, and working with the head office, the Sales Ambassador found a way to shorten the delay. So not only was the complaining customer satisfied, but others, some of whom were "tolerating" delays, suddenly became happier as well.

Sales Ambassadors see a complaint as golden. They are able to use it to turn a situation around. The customer is saying more than *"I am not happy."* She is giving the Sales Ambassador the chance to do something about it.

The approach to turning the situation around is to:

✦ Be receptive and use empathy.
✦ Acknowledge the complaint, adding, *"I understand."*
✦ Ask questions to clarify the situation.
✦ Propose immediate actions, stating, *"Here's what I'm going to do."*
✦ Take personal responsibility.
✦ Confirm the information with the customer.
✦ Thank the customer for bringing the situation to your attention.
✦ Follow up to ensure customer satisfaction.

Through listening, apologizing, and making a special gesture, the situation can be turned around. Often, the customer who has complained and goes away satisfied is more loyal than before.

Treasure complaints. Solving one can have a positive outcome for other customers.

The other *competitor*

18

The Sales Ambassador is well informed. He knows what the competitors are offering, and he knows what he can make as a counteroffer. He is also aware that there is another competitor and that this other competitor is just as serious as the other brands' proposals of similar models and creations.

Take three examples: a man coming in to look at a new car, a woman shopping for a new handbag, or a couple looking at a state-of-the-art home stereo and television system.

Do they really need to buy what they are looking at? Can he keep his old car a few more months or even another year? Is a new handbag absolutely essential at this time? Can the woman continue to use one of the (many) handbags she already has? Does the couple have to change their old but still functioning stereo and television?

The answer in each of these cases is *"They can wait!"*

The Sales Ambassador confronts a different kind of competitor than the store down the street. In all of the situations just mentioned, people could easily carry on without buying anything, at least for the moment. All three can walk out and, for the moment, have their lives remain pretty much the same.

So much can be determined by the Sales Ambassador. The first thing is to realize and recognize that not buying at all is a real option that needs to be addressed. We have talked about the importance of trying things on and trying things out. In each of these situations, the Sales Ambassador adds convincing arguments.

For the car, bringing up questions about reliability and security (not to mention the status of being seen driving it) can help persuade the potential buyer. What about the practicality of the size of the new handbag the woman is considering and how the color is highly fashionable? Or the pleasure the couple will have with the latest features available in the model they are considering and how they can invite friends and family over to enjoy their new system?

Every day people walk in with the option not to buy. Sales Ambassadors need to stay aware of this option.

Beware of the other competitor.

19

Service costs *nothing*

The Sales Ambassador is always looking for ways to advise customers and keep them happy. Offering a drink, having some candies for children, or suggesting ideas about how to give a gift are just some of the examples that are frequently used.

Customers appreciate advice from their Sales Ambassadors, such as helping with any needed servicing on their purchase or alerting them when something they have been looking for has arrived.

A Sales Ambassador's role is also to act like a "Concierge" in a hotel who is able to obtain a table in a popular restaurant or find tickets to a special exhibition.

A gesture of service is always appreciated.

20

The great *danger* of prejudices and preconceived ideas

"Clothes make the man" is a very dangerous expression, particularly in a sales situation. Sales Ambassadors have often told us stories that prove this expression to be false.

A young girl is looking at something in a showcase. A very plain looking couple is looking around, and an elderly gentleman with no visible luxury brand signs has entered the boutique.

Some dangerous mental statements sales associates might make are:

"She is too young to have money for anything expensive."

"That couple is not going to buy."

"There's no point in wasting my time on him."

However, in reality, the young girl has just inherited a fortune, the couple did not bother to dress up today, and the gentleman's brother is the CEO of one of China's biggest companies.

These examples are not exaggerated. They are the real stories Sales Ambassadors have experienced.

Treat every contact as a person you are eager to serve.

21

Work as a *team* player

Teams win over individuals, with team members sometimes supporting, sometimes being the main contact with the customer. Sales Ambassadors work hard at developing their skills to become effective team players.

A team communicates well. A team keeps the common goal in mind. The days go by faster in a positive and fun atmosphere. The pleasure of being together draws customers into the fun. When this happens, they want to come back.

Along with this, teams play an essential role in building the brand experience. Customers feel the positive flow of the team effort.

Customers can feel it when individuals are only looking out for their own interests in making the sale. This "everyone for himself" attitude is more than disagreeable. It is the cause of conflict, which, if not stopped, soon ruins the atmosphere of a store. When personal conflicts are in play, they sometimes become more important than customers, whose numbers dwindle.

Sales Ambassadors remember the importance of communication. Giving and sharing information goes a lot farther than keeping it to yourself.

Play your role in the team's success.

22

Relationships and mistakes

What happens when a boutique you've been going to for years makes a mistake, or the car stereo that is installed by your garage is not the one you ordered, or a restaurant you often go to forgets your reservation for lunch? Your first reaction may be anger. *"How could they?"*

Obviously a gesture of some kind is in order: a gift, a free-of-charge corrected order, or a bottle of wine the next time you're in the restaurant to express that they too are upset that they did not come through for you.

When the relationship is solid, we forgive. We're all human and we all make mistakes. This gives us an opportunity for a little humor, and life goes on. The situation is smoothed over and, of course, avoided in the future.

Sales Ambassadors are not always responsible for errors or decisions made by the brand, for example, a repair that was promised to be finished by a certain date, a faulty item that somehow made it past quality control, or an unanticipated price increase that leaves the customer furious.

For customers, the Sales Ambassador is their contact, so their frustration is directed at him. This always calls for diplomacy, and the ability to deal calmly with the customer's anger and frustration.

Sales Ambassadors tell us that in several instances some of their best customers were, in the past, some of their most angry customers over a specific incident. By using their ability to deal with the negative situation in an understanding and positive way, those Sales Ambassadors were able to keep them as customers. Even when a customer left the boutique with smoke coming out of his ears, a note, a bouquet of flowers, a request to see him again was often all it took to reestablish contact.

The ability to say "I understand, and I'm sorry" will help you keep customers.

Story 2

After entering the luxury boutique, the client was warmly greeted and offered a seat. He immediately took out a leather watch strap and explained to the Sales Ambassador that he was unhappy with it. To many Sales Associates, this kind of intervention is often seen as a waste of time. Not by the Sales Ambassador in this situation, who saw the customer contact as an opportunity. She noticed the watch the customer was wearing and complimented him on it. And what other timepieces did he have? In just a few minutes, she learned that he owned several watches. She ordered coffee, and they continued to discuss his collection. She extended the discussion, "Are you aware of our new platinum watch that has just been launched?" Out came a wonderful selection for him to look at.

How do you think this concluded? See page 149.

Part Three: The *Savoir-Faire* of the Sales Ambassador

Asia was the first place to speak of shopping as a hobby. But once customers step inside a boutique, something magical needs to happen. This is when the Sales Ambassador becomes the brand for the customer. Together, they share the pleasure and celebration of beautiful creations that luxury fashion offers.

—*Jean Lahirle*
Managing Director,
Celine, Asia-Pacific

23 The successful *selling style*

What is a successful selling style? Here is our definition:

Skills and abilities that a Sales Ambassador has acquired that provide customers with solutions to their needs and that also creates a desire to return and experience the same pleasure again.

Sales Ambassadors know that they have an active role to play in a sale. The object in and of itself is not all there is in providing a solution. The art of selling is more complex than simply pulling something off the shelf, ringing it up, putting it in a bag, muttering *"Thank You,"* and moving on to the next customer. If this were all there was to it, robots could do the job. They could even be programmed to say *"Thank you"* with an added *"Have a nice day"* at the end.

The second part of the definition is just as important. Each contact should be one in which the exchange create the desire not only to purchase this time but to continue to return to do the same again in the future. The Sales Ambassador is constantly approaching the sale in a way that encourages the customer to come back. Once again, establishing a person-to-person relationship plays an important role in finding out about customer needs and building loyalty.

Successful selling requires an approach that is both immediate and long term.

24 Life is a *celebration*

Why do people purchase? One of the main reasons has to do with celebrating life's events. People want to show others how much they mean to them. There is often a party or get together of friends and family to share these moments.

The occasions fall into two major categories:

1. **Yearly events** such as Valentine's Day, Mother's and Father's day, religious celebrations, or New Year's.
2. **Personal life/Family events:** the birth of a child, birthdays, graduations, engagements, weddings, promotions, or anniversaries.

The Sales Ambassador anticipates the yearly events and contacts customers ahead of time to order or reserve gifts they might need. Using the customer file, the Sales Ambassador reminds customers of personal events, just in case they may have forgotten and of course, when appropriate:

"You know, Valentine's Day is just around the corner. . . ."
"Isn't your wedding anniversary in a month's time?"
"Wouldn't it be nice if he received something after working so hard at finishing his studies?"

Sales Ambassadors have told us that the service provided in reminding and helping customers pick out gifts is very much appreciated, especially from busy customers who no longer remember what they bought the previous years and of course want to avoid buying the same thing.

Every occasion is an opportunity to help your customer celebrate life.

25

Use each contact to *inform* and *educate*

People are usually open and even eager to learn new things when the opportunity is presented in an appropriate way. Sales Ambassadors have the opportunity to educate with each customer contact, and the learning experience, whether there is a purchase or not, is very much appreciated.

People are often fascinated by knowledge. Here are a few examples:

+ **Diamonds are a miracle of Nature and were formed 50 million years ago.**

+ **It takes 10 years of experience to be a professional jewelry polisher.**

+ **The champagne the couple is interested in has been creating sparkling wines for 250 years.**

+ **Wearing a wedding band on your fourth finger has to do with a vein in that finger that goes directly to the heart.**

+ **A wristwatch dates back to less than a century ago.**

+ **This watch was selected to be worn on the first visit to the moon.**

Sales Ambassadors are aware of the power of learning during a sale and find ways to educate with each contact they make.

Sharing knowledge creates bonds between you and your customers.

26 The *Power of timing*

Timing is the art of knowing the right moment to do or say something. Timing touches all aspects of our lives. You can move too quickly or not fast enough. Each person operates at different rhythms. An approach that is much too fast for one individual may be too slow for another. What is slow for one customer could be too pushy for someone else.

Customers who have just come into the boutique (of course after being greeted and acknowledged) often need to get into the atmosphere for a few moments before having any conversations or exchanges with a Sales Ambassador.

Timing does not only come with experience. It comes with an ability to observe and "feel" each situation. It is also the understanding that the timing will be different each time. Each new element changes the timing.

Timing can be seen from several angles:

✦ **Offering time:** People from certain cultures need more time to reflect and select what they want to purchase.

✦ **Offering silence:** In certain situations saying nothing encourages the customer to speak and therefore give you valuable clues.

✦ **Timing in making a choice:** Questions such as *"How do you feel about this model?"* asked at the right time by the Sales Ambassador will help focus the sale.

◆ **Offering alternatives:** Knowing when to propose another option when the Sales Ambassador feels the customer may want to see something else.

◆ **Timing to conclude:** When the Sales Ambassador sees that the customer is pleased with the offer, a sincere compliment to move to purchase.

Each time is different, making timing one of the most fascinating aspects of selling.

Watch closely and "feel" each situation's uniqueness.

Time is a *precious* sales tool

27

Situation 1: A couple is considering a serious purchase.

Situation 2: An appealing proposal goes well over a customer's budget.

Situation 3: A customer has discovered a beautiful piece that she was not even considering owning a few moments earlier.

What do these three situations require? They all need a little time. Time to reflect for a moment on an investment that is made complex by emotion and desire.

Sales Ambassadors understand that rushing or being pushy can run the risk of losing an opportunity. They take a step back and observe while still remaining available. They may even leave the customer alone for a while to reflect.

People often talk about *"taking time"* for something. It is more about giving time than taking it. While the world outside is in a terrible hurry, in the boutique, the Sales Ambassador shows she has time to listen, explain, or simply be there in the silence with the customer.

Giving the situation time builds trust, an essential in any relationship. Time also allows the customer to feel the pleasure of ownership.

Situation 1: The couple may need some additional information.

Situation 2: The person with a budget issue will appreciate time to think about how he will cover the extra investment.

Situation 3: Someone considering a new creation may need time to imagine herself wearing the creation and the compliments she will have.

But before any of this happens comes the moment to give customers time alone or with each other to let time play its role.

To make the sale and build the relationship, give time.

The art of using *silence*

28

We have seen that with each customer contact, there is a time for everything. There is a time to greet and a time to discover. There is a time to explain and a time to respond to questions that the customer might have.

There is also a time for silence. *"Know how to listen and know that the silence produces the same effect as science,"* Napoleon said. The same applies to the silence in a sales situation.

Often, silence leaves a void that people fill with their conversation. This information can be very valuable for a Sales Ambassador. Interpreting the silence is important and being able to answer questions such as *"Are there any other explanations I need to make?"* or *"Is there any doubt in the customer's mind?"* If the answer is "No," then there is still time to stay in the silence.

Silence has an elegance to it, a moment of being present, perhaps giving the person time to think something through or to take the situation into consideration. The necessary information has been shared, and the Sales Ambassador leaves the silence there, undisturbed.

Silence cuts through the noise and chatter that increasingly surround us.

To help the sale, leave space for the silence.

Music as a *metaphor* for selling

29

Selling has many things in common with playing a musical instrument. Both require a lot of practice and preparation before a performance. The selling environment can be very much like being a jazz musician. At some moments, there are clear structures and rules to follow. At other moments, improvisation, relying on feeling the moment as much as possible, is needed.

The Sales Ambassador is very much aware of the need to follow certain guidelines, yet to remain flexible. There are moments when she needs to take the lead, knowing that when the customer indicates something else, the sales process must take another direction. Within the pattern of listening, discovering, and proposing, the art of improvisation often needs to take place.

While the main phases of a sale need to be respected, a customer may simply not be interested in certain aspects. The next customer may find that same point fascinating, and want to spend a lot more time discussing and learning more. With each situation, the Sales Ambassador needs to feel where the process is going, flow with the information she is picking up from the customer, and adapt.

Practice and prepare.
But be ready to improvise.

$Select$ the words you use $carefully$

30

The words used are keys to conveying a message. When they are well chosen, they help the Sales Ambassador communicate the beauty of emotion. When specific well-selected words are used, the listener wants to hear more.

Some words and phrases are simply more positive and elegant than others. They serve as a vehicle to enhance the subject being discussed. *"Sushi"* sounds a lot better than *"raw fish."* The word *"product"* does not have the same magic as *"creation."*

With words there is often a choice that needs to be made to express an additional quality. Choosing one over the other takes the discussion into another universe.

"We are going to find a piece that your wife will really love" has much more impact than simply saying, *"I will find you something."*

Instead of *"price"* or *"cost,"* try *"value."* Choose *"unique"* over *"different"* and *"exquisite"* over *"nice."*

The right words add value to the proposal and make it more intense.

31

Tones, rhythms, and *volumes*

What is it about certain voices that make them such a pleasure to listen to? There is the emotional quality, the joy and happiness they express. There is a tone that can vary from warm and sensual to exciting and wonderful. There is a rhythm, or speed of delivery, that accelerates, slows down, or stretches to hold our interest.

The Sales Ambassador is an actor. The boutique is his stage. The verbal exchanges with his customer are his "lines." One of the key aspects of an actor's craft is how he develops the character of his voice. In the same performance, he may need to laugh, cry, express anger, fall in love, scream, and whisper. Each change in emotion requires different tones, rhythms, and volumes.

Sales Ambassadors do many things to improve their voices, such as speaking in a warm tone rather than mumbling or using an inappropriate tone. The very act of smiling while speaking also gives a pleasant aspect to your voice.

Sales Ambassadors know it requires a conscious effort on their part to improve, especially in the beginning. They study and practice in order to have a better vocal quality. These "rehearsals" can also use the "scripts" of key words and phrases taken from everyday sales situations.

Develop the pleasant qualities in the sound of your voice.

The competition, your customers, and your *advantages*

32

People shop around. We love to compare. The shopping experience would not exist if there were no alternatives.

A Sales Ambassador knows this. Regardless of what he is selling, he is aware of what could tempt his potential customer elsewhere. He does not simply study a photograph in a magazine or read a product review. He goes and finds out, firsthand, until he knows what the competition is doing.

In other words, he goes shopping.

If he is selling cars, he goes and drives the models of his competitors and studies their performance ratings. If it is a fashion brand, the Sales Ambassador knows not only the colors the jacket comes in, but the details such as pockets and zippers as well. She has tried on the shoes and the coats and touched the materials they are made of. If it is high tech, he knows the characteristics of the competitor's models by heart.

In each case, the Sales Ambassador develops one thing: knowledge that helps him present the advantages of each offer. Knowledge reassures and helps the customer decide.

Fine-tune your added value in relation to the competitor's offer.

Personalize your service

33

One of our customers returned to a prestigious hotel in Boston after having been away for two years. As he approached the counter, the receptionist looked at him with a big smile and said *"Welcome back, Mr. Dupont."*

"You remembered my name?"

"I verified your flight arrival and calculated the time it would take for you to get here. Would you like your wake-up call the same as on your last visit?"

After a pause,

"Ah, what time was that?"
"7:30."
"That will be fine."
"And the Financial Times again this time, Mr. Dupont?"
"Yes, yes that would be fine."

People like personalized services. They prefer to be loyal to Sales Ambassadors who care about them and remember their preferences.

In personalization, you are often competing with prestigious hotels.

Pleasure comes from

consistency

34

Each Sales Ambassador has answers to the question: *"What do your customers expect from you?"* Once the list is made, then the Sales Team works on solutions to the question, *"What can we do to make sure that these expectations are consistently met?"*

Consistency is a major aspect in building customer loyalty. There should be no rude surprises. The Sales Ambassador wants to hear:

"Every time I call them, they help me."

"I can count on them to come through when they say they will."

"The quality of their service is always superb."

"She is always friendly."

Everyone on the Sales Team needs to be sensitive to and participate in consistency. It is a fundamental on which Sales Ambassadors build their reputations. Without it, they are hit-and-miss salespeople promoting a hit-and-miss brand.

Build on consistency and you will already be ahead of most of your competitors.

35

Maintain your *energy*

Selling can be physically draining. On a crowded day, with a busy store, each member of the Sales Team walks miles back and forth, up and down stairs. When the afternoon comes, legs begin to feel heavy, and arms are also tired from reaching and putting things away.

There is a mental fatigue as well, from answering questions, running to the telephone, and dealing diplomatically with specific customer requests.

Customers have a tendency to show up at the same time, in waves. A store may be completely empty for hours, and then for some reason, it fills up, with everyone busy and people waiting, sometimes impatiently, to be served.

Regardless of when they arrive, whether it is at the opening, their lunch break, or at the end of the day, customers want and deserve a Sales Ambassador who is happy to see them and wanting to help.

To balance and share the workload, Sales Ambassadors truly work as team members. They take breaks when things are slower or during down times. When possible they go outside, get some fresh air, and sit somewhere to get off their feet. They have a drink and listen to music. In some stores, massage chairs have been installed.

Staggering arrivals and departures for the team can also be important to keeping a good level of energy. Who likes to come in early, so that they can leave earlier? Who would like to show up a little later and stay until closing?

All of these require reflection and understanding between the Sales Ambassadors and the manager. At the same time, Sales Ambassadors never forget that a customer should always meet a fresh and smiling face regardless of when they visit.

Work together with the team to pace yourself.

Make someone's day

36

Sales Ambassadors depend on each other for having a successful day. But what about their managers? How can the team help make the manager's day? What responsibilities can Sales Ambassadors take on to lighten the workload of a manager? There is much to be learned by having tasks delegated from the manager. Taking on tasks frees the manager to deal with other priorities. This can only add to the success of the boutique.

What about other departments working directly with the Sales Team in the company? How can you make their day be as pleasurable as possible? What about your telephone contacts with other company members and suppliers?

Build a reputation of being someone ready and willing to help. Optimists and positive people not only live longer, they have happier lives. They are also people others like being around. Remember also that today someone needs your help, and tomorrow you may have a special request or need for which they would be willing to go out of their way.

Go ahead. Make their day.

Each telephone contact

37 is another *opportunity*

People "let their fingers do the walking" and call stores to inquire about the availability of specific items and also about prices. Some boutiques refuse to give prices over the telephone. In those cases, the Sales Ambassador invites the caller to come by in person for more information or offers to make a special appointment to discuss the item in question.

A Sales Ambassador uses the telephone contact to discover as much as possible about the person who has called. In most professional situations today, when a Sales Ambassador answers a call, he automatically gives the name of the brand and his name. The voice on the telephone should always be warm, pleasant, and welcoming. Kindness and courtesy come through loud and clear because the voice is standing alone. The objective here is to succeed in having the caller come into the store.

A few questions concerning the request from the caller will give valuable information:

"Would you mind telling me how you discovered this model?"

"Could I find out a little more about the occasion so that I can assist you in your choice?"

Remembering the emotional side of purchasing is also important and should be communicated over the telephone. Descriptions of shapes and colors need vivid exciting language if the Sales Ambassador is going to succeed in convincing the potential customer to come into the boutique.

What if the caller is still not convinced to come by? Offer to send a catalog. This way, the address is in your file for future reference.

Always make sure that the potential customers are thanked for their call and that every effort has been made to make them feel that they are welcome to call again or to come by anytime.

Turn each telephone inquiry into a positive experience.

Analyze
the sale you made

38

"What was the last sale you made?" It is an easy question for a Sales Ambassador to answer. A more complex one is *"Why do you think the customer made the purchase?"* The answer to this question reveals a great deal about a Sales Ambassador's ability to understand and analyze a sale, as well as the customer's buying habits. People buy things for a variety of reasons.

Sometimes an object will sell itself. The customer simply wanted to possess the popular item:

"She came in, asked to see the model, and that was all there was to it."

A lack of time can also trigger a sale. A person only has an hour at lunch to find a gift for someone that same evening. Here, the honest answer from the Sales Ambassador would be:

"He was in a hurry. After I showed him the first item, he asked if it could be gift wrapped quickly. When I said 'Yes,' he took out his credit card."

In both cases, the Sales Ambassadors played their roles and adapted to the needs of the customers. Even in these quick sale situations, they still are aware of the opportunity of the contact and use the moment to establish the beginning of a relationship.

Of course, most sales are not as simple as these examples. In some cases, a customer will come back several times before deciding to purchase. Here, a different set of skills is called on in order to succeed. Selling in this situation can be very rewarding:

"I didn't give up. He came in three times to see the creation. This morning, he came in and purchased it. He told me the reason he bought the piece was that I had established a link between him and the creation."

Analyzing a sale helps Sales Ambassadors see differences between when they are really selling and when they are politely ringing up purchases that happen with little effort on their part.

Evaluate your sales to reinforce your skills.

Analyze the situation when the customer did *not buy*

39

Just as important as analyzing why someone has made a purchase is also analyzing a situation where someone did not do so. An alert Sales Ambassador will be able to answer the question, *"Why do you think the customer left without buying?"*

Someone has visited the boutique and has left empty handed. It would, of course, be unfair to say that everyone leaving who does not buy is a lost sale. Sometimes, the person was simply not going to purchase. Or someone may have only been interested in obtaining information.

It could also be a question of stock or something missing from the brand's offer. In these types of situations, it is important to let the company know.

But a lost sale may also be because of something that did not happen between the Sales Associate and the customer. Sales Ambassadors make sure they are not losing sales because of their approach. The following questions can help evaluate a lost sale.

+ **What took place during the exchanges we had that did not go well?**

+ **What would I do differently during a similar situation in the future?**

+ **Who could help me with learning and practicing these skills?**

Evaluate why customers leave without buying.

Story 3

The telephone today remains a powerful selling tool when used effectively. In one situation, a customer called the boutique to get information on a specific creation. During the discussion over the telephone, the Sales Ambassador invited the customer to come by and see the piece. The customer explained that he was unable to come in because he was not well. The Sales Ambassador asked if he had a computer in his home, which he did. They both connected to the Brand's web site and continued their conversation, this time with beautiful visuals to go along with the explanations.

How do you think this concluded? See page 149.

Part Four: Preparing to Sell

A day of selling is not much different from a theater play. In both cases, rehearsing and preparation are crucial: lines to learn, a stage to set up, an atmosphere to create, a Director's comments to take into consideration, with a unique goal—an audience to enthrall. All things considered, a day of selling is much more difficult than a part in a play. In a boutique, the entire cast is doomed to excellence because there will not be any second chances. On top of this, each and every Sales Ambassador must play both the leading part and the supporting role to assist other colleagues. Last, but not least, the Sales Team must improvise a new role for each and every new customer, while never forgetting that the show must go on, whatever happens.

—Laurence Nicolas
Director, Jewelry Division
Christian Dior

The impact of the right
atmosphere on customers

40

Ever walked into a boutique or store and walked right back out again? What happened?

Something just did not feel right to you. Was it the whispering Sales Associates deep in discussion of an obviously personal matter who hardly acknowledged your entrance? Was it the lighting (or lack of it) or music that was too loud or inappropriate? Was it a certain disorder that was confusing and unappealing? Was it the un-cleanliness or the strong odor of a cleaning product that someone had just used?

Or was it a mixture of things, which brought you to the point of letting your feet decide that this place was not for you?

Achieving the right atmosphere does more than create an environment in which it is a pleasure to work and receive customers.

It also increases sales.

Creating and keeping the right atmosphere is part of a Sales Ambassador's job. What makes your space unique? Are you after an intimate warmth, a brightness, or a cool lifestyle effect? How can you create a uniqueness for your space so that the senses are awakened the moment a person steps into your store's universe?

It all adds up to an atmosphere so that when people enter they want to linger. The place is an immediate experience, with a feeling brought on by the lighting, the music, the colors, the smells, and perhaps, the offer of a drink or some chocolate.

When the experience is right, customers will come back to have it again.

Take a step back. Listen, look, smell, touch, even taste the atmosphere.

Luxury is in the *details*

41

Outside the boutique, you notice that the main external display has an empty space where something has been removed. Because it is raining, the floor at the main entrance is starting to look muddy from the wet foot traffic. Inside, a child with sticky hands has run her fingers across the front of the glass display counter. Someone has left a Kleenex and a used coffee cup on one of the tables.

Are these just a few details? Well yes. But while each and every aspect may not seem like much, the accumulation says something that negatively affects the image of the boutique and the brand.

The Sales Ambassador is often the first to notice these small but important details, and she moves quickly to improve the situation. Knowing that small but unacceptable things can soon create a nonluxurious atmosphere, she keeps a constant vigilance.

The little things matter.
Pay attention to the details.

Keep the service level up even when things are *busy*

42

As we said earlier, customers can arrive in waves, from no one in the store for hours to, suddenly, many people needing assistance at once. This phenomenon often causes customers to become irritated and puts pressure on the sales staff who are trying to do their best.

People grow impatient when the instant gratification they are used to is not there. Because of this, when they have to wait, their expectations of the service become even higher than they would normally be.

Sales Ambassadors are sensitive to this issue. If there are customers coming in who are obviously not happy with the crowd in the store, they are still greeted and offered an apology. Sometimes the suggestion, ***"Could you possibly come by a little later?"*** may be made, or when appropriate, the Sales Ambassador may propose an appointment.

If the customer is going to be in the same area for a while and wants to give her cell phone number, the Sales Ambassador can contact her when the boutique is a little quieter.

What could be available in the boutique while people are waiting? Magazines and catalogs, and if space permits, there should be places to sit as well. A proposal of something to drink is an option to consider. Some boutiques are also offering their customers Internet access and a telephone and even cell phone charging stations. What about providing games and toys for children?

Many boutiques are also hiring a doorman to make the first impression very positive. Of course he should be friendly, and being handsome also helps.

When people have waited and are finally being served, the Sales Ambassador should always offer a second apology. It is also important to thank customers for their patience once again when they leave.

Can busy times be anticipated? Certainly some of them can. Sales Ambassadors have an excellent opportunity for contacting their customers to set appointments during quieter times.

Customer service expectations are higher during busy times.

Prepare your *selling tools*

43

For a day of selling, Sales Ambassadors need a number of items available at their fingertips. When a customer comes in, any break to look for something disturbs the contact.

What are your tools? Are they all within reach and ready to be used? A calculator with a dead battery, an outdated catalog, or a polishing cloth that is dirty means going into the back room and digging through drawers.

The customer expects a professional, not a disorganized person. When everything is easily available, the Sales Ambassador can concentrate on making the sale.

Being organized also saves time; the smoother the contact is, the more likely the sale will take place.

Before the boutique opens,
make sure your tools are ready.

Know what you have
in *stock*

44

Each day, before opening, the Sales Ambassador needs to verify which pieces and sizes are in the boutique and which ones are unavailable. Knowing this not only saves time, but also makes it easier for the Sales Ambassador to stay with the customer. It avoids having to go into the back to search, only to return with nothing.

Knowing what is not available also makes it easier for the Sales Ambassador to prepare alternative offers. If this is not suitable for the customer, does another store have the piece in stock? Can it be sent over? Can it be available later today or tomorrow? If it is sold out and unavailable elsewhere, how long will it take to have one ordered? Would the customer like you to contact her when the specific model does come in? Would she like you to deliver the piece to her home?

During the day as well, when a Sales Ambassador sells the last piece of a specific model, he should inform the other team members. This way information is constantly updated. Arrivals of pieces should also be communicated.

Knowing what is in stock and offering alternative solutions when items are not available enhances the professional image of a Sales Ambassador.

Be aware of what is available and which alternative offers to propose.

Learn how each creation was crafted

45

Sales Ambassadors continuously increase their knowledge about what they are selling. Who designed it? What inspired it? What are the identifiable specific aspects of the piece? How was it made? How many people were involved in making it? What is the history behind the creation? What are the features that make it unique?

The Sales Ambassador uses this knowledge when adapting her presentation during a sale. From this pool of information she chooses an approach that arouses the customer's interest and brings the sale to a successful close.

Selling is not simply a question of handing over an object and taking the money. As customers, we like to know that our purchase goes beyond a simple practical aspect. We want to be more informed about the work, creativity, and reflection that went into the making of the piece.

Where do Sales Ambassadors go to obtain information? First of all, the brand usually informs staff about new creations. But the Sales Ambassador should take it one or sometimes two steps further. Many sources abound that give valuable information: specialty magazines, the web, books, catalogs, and editorials, to name a few.

Stay informed about what your brand is offering.

Know *what is happening* in your city

46

A few years ago, a newly hired Sales Ambassador for a luxury brand was selling a higher volume than several senior members of the sales staff. We took him to lunch to find out more about his approach. Perhaps it was simply beginner's luck.

It turned out that one of the things he did systematically, whether the person purchased or not, was to share with customers what was happening in his city. He commented that whether he made the sale or not on their first visit, they often came back later to see him and to purchase. He noticed too that they would send friends.

Establishing a person-to-person relationship can sometimes be accomplished by being a source of information for your customers. Whether they are locals or foreigners, it is important to let them know about a new restaurant that has just opened, an exhibition or interesting sites they should see or visit in the area.

Other Sales Ambassadors have confirmed how important this is in making and keeping customer contact. Once again, it reaffirms your personal interest in the customer.

Sales Ambassadors' personal networks help them stay informed of what's going on in the area, and they often take it one step further. They keep a small stock of maps of the city and local guides to exhibits and specific shows that are playing.

Share your list of great places to go and things to do with your customers.

Story 4

The Sales Ambassador of a prestigious champagne brand
learned that The Rolling Stones had just released a new CD.
She remembered how one of her customers was a die-hard
fan of the Stones. Going through her customer file, she
quickly found the customer's name and the carefully noted
anecdote about the Stones.

How do you think this concluded? See page 149.

Part Five: Welcoming and Discovering the Customer

Selling a Lexus is very different from selling other brands of cars. Building a relationship is more complex than before. Customers are looking for a different kind of statement. They want a lifestyle, an extension of their personality. Lexus has its own approach: to astonish customers each and every time they come into contact with the brand.

—Eric Bousseffa
Sales Ambassador,
Lexus France

A *greeting* needs a *smile*

47

"Never open a shop if you don't know how to smile," the Middle East expression goes. We extend this idea to anyone working in sales: *"Forget about selling if you cannot smile."*

A smile is more than just the visual effort from the face to push up the corners of the mouth. It needs at least a couple of drops of sincerity to work. Adding a simple expression to it such as *"Welcome"* delivered warmly makes it complete.

A smile is the sign of an optimist, and optimism is contagious. In other words, when you feel good and smile, you pass this effect on to others. As human beings, we want to spend time with people who make us feel good and in places where we feel welcomed and comfortable.

Smiling is also universal. It crosses all borders and cultures. Sales Associates sometimes mention that they know little or nothing about the cultures of people from foreign countries or of different ethnicities who come into their stores. But they already have a powerful tool they can use that creates a contact and a positive beginning: a smile. It works with the person across the street or across the world.

A smile puts the customer at ease, and it does not cost a thing!

Smile!

48

Your *body language* speaks louder than words

The saleswoman is leaning on a wall and has her arms and legs crossed as you walk in. She makes the smallest of smiles and mutters a hardly audible *"Hello"* while still maintaining her knotted up position. She makes no move toward you, and you have no desire to go near her. Everything about her is shouting, ***"Leave me alone!"***

In another area, a salesman says ***"Of course, Madam"*** but then lets out a loud sigh and rolls his eyes because the woman wants to try on another model.

Another Sales Associate is having a discussion with a customer who obviously has a complaint. As he listens, he puts up his hands in an unspoken gesture that translates to ***"Shut up, I've heard enough!"*** It should be no surprise that the customer becomes even more irritated.

Okay, this is at the end of a busy sales day, but so what? Is it the customer's fault that this is the only time he could come by? Why should he be receiving a different level of service?

Study after study indicates that if your body language is in contradiction with what you are saying, people believe what they see.

Keep your hands by your sides, use open palm gestures, and keep your legs uncrossed. Stand up straight and use eye contact that is appropriate. Your body, gestures, and eye contact should be telling the customers that you are available and listening, ready to wait on them.

Watch what your body language and gestures are saying.

Listening with your *eyes*

49

Every day people walk into stores telling their stories before they speak. Here are three examples:

1. **A couple** comes in, the man has his arm around her, and they share a quick intimate moment. They move through the store together, holding hands.

2. **A woman alone** wanders through the store, looking at objects in the displays. For a few moments, she stares intently at one specific piece.

3. **A woman and a young teenage girl** come in together. The girl has her head down, arms across her chest, and does not respond to the woman, who is proposing things to her.

Through observation, the Sales Ambassador can prepare the contact from a distance. This is why having an adaptable selling style is essential.

Along with observing behavior, what people wear can give valuable clues. The situation with the couple is based on a real situation. The Sales Ambassador noticed that the woman was wearing pink diamond earrings. During the discovery phase, the Sales Ambassador learned that they had come to buy an overcoat for the man. But the observation of the pink earrings created the opportunity to also propose and sell an haute couture pink dress to the woman.

Of course, as we have already discussed, it is necessary to avoid preconceived notions about customers. Nevertheless, through observation, much information is often gained.

Customers may give you valuable information from the moment you are able to observe them.

50

The importance
of *discovery*

At first glance, they look like any other customers. Three people have walked into three different stores. Mike is looking for a new suit, Susan wants a new car, and Ron is looking for a gift.

But under the surface, many things are happening. Mike wants a smart suit that will help him succeed in a very important job interview that is coming up. He wants to wear something that will impress as well as make him feel comfortable and relaxed.

Susan wants a new car. Even though she may not look like it (it is Saturday, and she is dressed casually), she has just been promoted and is now CEO of her company. The company will provide her with the car of her choice.

Ron wants to buy a gift for his girlfriend to mark the two years they have been together. He's unsure what to get her, but doesn't want to encourage any mistaken engagement hopes.

Discovery lets the Sales Ambassador know what is behind each purchase, which in turn assists him in helping the customer make the right choice. A few simple open questions or statements along with careful observation gives the information needed to provide the best solution:

"Tell me about the occasion."
"Is there an important date/event?"
"Tell me more about your preferences?"
"What creations does she already own?"
"What do you like about our brand?"

For Mike's suit, knowing a little more about the company interviewing him could also guide the purchase. Is it a conservative type of company or a hip place where something more casual would be acceptable?

In the case of the car, knowing that Susan's company is paying for the car opens different options.

For Ron, the Sales Ambassador needs to know what other types of jewelry his girlfriend already owns and wears, some of her likes and dislikes, and her preferences and style of dressing.

People are buying much more than the object.

51

The *Gift Purchase*

When a customer comes to purchase a gift, the Sales Ambassador uses a very specific approach:

"Thank you for thinking of us for this gift! Please, tell me more about the occasion."

Why start by thanking them for coming? Any brand should feel honored about being considered as a source for a gift. Discovering the occasion in a discreet and warm way adds value to the contact and opens the door to appropriate suggestions.

In talking about the occasion, the Sales Ambassador is also informed about who will be receiving the gift and when. With the next questions asked, the Sales Ambassador should find out as much as possible about this person's tastes, the pieces she already owns, and when the gift would be worn or used. Again, important information can help with the proposal.

Before proposing anything, thank the customer for choosing your brand.

The power of questions
(quality over quantity)

52

Questions are powerful tools for the Sales Ambassador. They go beyond the salesperson/customer roles and into establishing the person-to-person relationship. Open questions starting with What, How, Why, Which, and Where are most effective when discovering.

What happens if they are not used? Look at the following example that you can also try on a group of friends.

In seventeenth century France, Charles, a member of the royal court, awoke one night to the noise of robbers who had succeeded in climbing over the protective wall and were passing through his bedroom to rob precious treasures from his castle. The robbers made several trips through Charles's bedroom, each time carrying another precious art object with them.

But Charles said nothing while all of this happened. In the morning, when it was discovered that the thieves had gone through his bedroom he also said nothing. Why?

The answer is quite simple, but in most cases, people will either make statements (guess) or use closed questions. For example:

"Because he was afraid."

"Was it so dark he could not see their faces?"

"Was he blind?"

But the riddle can be solved with a one simple open question:

"What can you tell me about Charles?"

Well, the answer is that he was a baby, only nine months old, when the robbery took place.

Sales Ambassadors use open questions to uncover pertinent information they need to understand about the customer and his universe. Open questions help Sales Ambassadors save time in selecting a proposal. They also know that when it comes time to conclude, their investment in discovery helps them close the sale.

When talking about preferences, either/or questions work well; when concluding, closed questions are ideal.

The Sales Ambassador realizes that she needs to emphasize quality over quantity. The contact with a customer should never become an interrogation. If this happens, it could be so irritating that the customer may walk out.

When questioning your customers, use quality over quantity.

Be a *careful* listener

53

Selling is more about listening and observing than talking. The Sales Ambassador knows that a lot of information is learned through letting the customer tell his story.

There is an elegance in listening that should be remembered. Sales Ambassadors show that they are listening by making eye contact, nodding, and by using small words of agreement or surprise at what the customer is saying. At first, these may seem to be very small gestures, but they are vital in assuring customers that the Sales Ambassador is present and interested.

Active listening is more than simply shutting your mouth. It requires awareness and the ability to interpret. When the Sales Ambassador listens, the customer reveals himself.

To know your customer, activate your listening.

Find out how your customer *feels* about your brand

54

We have already mentioned that Sales Ambassadors learn a lot about the competition by going out and educating themselves. There is another often-overlooked approach that is just as important. It works particularly well when the Sales Ambassador has successfully established a person-to-person contact. It has to do with simply asking the customer:

"I notice you are wearing one of our creations. Tell me, what do you like about our brand?"

"Before we take a look at some pieces of our collection, what is important for you in this purchase?"

"Tell me, what have you seen elsewhere that you like?"

There are, of course, variations on these that also work well. In most cases, the customer is more than happy to share with you what she has seen, what she likes, and what is important for her. This valuable information, along with knowledge of the competitor, helps win the sale.

To target the advantages of your offer, find out what the customer is thinking and feeling.

Make *statements* to obtain information

55

We have covered the importance of discovering your customer and how it is an essential key to the success of a sale. We've discussed how you can obtain information by observing and by asking questions.

A third way to effective discovery is the "open-statement" approach:

"What a lovely accent you have."

In many cases, the customer will then tell you where he comes from. This, then, could become an immense area for other questions and discussions about his country of origin.

Using an open statement is saying something that encourages the customer to react and speak. It can be useful when you feel that questions might seem to be too probing to your customers.

If you see a customer in front of a window where many blue clothes are displayed, you could say:

"It seems you like blue." or *"I see that you have noticed something in particular in the window."*

Her reaction gives you valuable information.

The "open-statement" approach can provide you with many opportunities to gain knowledge about your customers.

Introduce yourself

56

Customers give you clues about how they want to be treated and how quickly they can build trust with you. At one moment or another, it may feel right to introduce yourself. Sales Ambassadors develop the ability to know when the timing is right.

Giving your name must come across as being information you would like them to have on a person-to-person level. Knowing someone's name is also part of building trust and loyalty:

"Let me show you some of our collection. By the way, my name is Lara."

If you offer your name and there is little reaction or the customer never uses your name, then it is best to leave it at that. Sometimes customers will give you their names. This means that they are also into establishing a friendly contact with you.

Offering customers your business card is another way of letting them know who you are. Another option for the Sales Ambassador to present herself comes when concluding or when the customer is about to leave:

"Let me give you my card. I am Lara James, and please feel free to contact me for any information you might need."

Once again, by doing this and watching the reaction, a Sales Ambassador might request a card from the customer.

Look for clues.
Find the right moment to introduce yourself.

57

"Just looking"

An Asian couple walks into a boutique and as soon as they are greeted, nervously respond, *"Just looking, just looking."* The Sales Ambassador gives them a welcoming smile, with a hand and arm gesture inviting them to look wherever they wish.

While certain nationalities use *"Just looking"* more than others (it is even written out phonetically in certain tourist guidebooks), it remains one of the most-often heard expressions in a boutique. Like the expression "Let me think about it," "Just looking" can mean many things.

Here are some of the most common:

"Please let us browse without having a sales associate pressuring us to buy."

"As we do not have anything specific in mind, we'd like to search on our own."

"We are afraid to ask specific questions."

The physical space between the Sales Ambassador and the customer should be appropriate so that the customer feels that she has freedom of movement yet that the Sales Ambassador is still available when needed.

There often comes a moment when the *"Just looking"* customer is finished wandering around and stops in front of one specific display (the customer may have already passed by it once, and has now returned). This is a signal for the Sales Ambassador to close the space and move into a dialogue:

"The piece you are looking at is part of our new collection. The design is based on a unique model that was made in the 1930s."

"What piece would you like to try on?"

Customers who come in with the intention of looking around do end up making purchases. Their decision to buy is often due to the atmosphere in the boutique and the ability of the Sales Ambassador to quickly establish a relationship.

Sales Ambassadors have even gone outside their boutiques to talk to customers looking at the window displays. A smile and a warm invitation to come inside have often led to a sale.

See every "Just looking" customer as an opportunity.

58

The art and importance
of *reformulation*

Before making a proposal, the Sales Ambassador reformulates the information he has learned during the discovery. He may decide to use the keywords spoken by the customer or paraphrase what he has picked up.

Reformulation is a great tool to use for many reasons. It indicates to the customer that you have listened and understood. It creates a context for rapid agreement and shows the customer that his opinion counts. It also saves time and makes the proposal easier:

"So if I understand, you are looking for an evening handbag for your wife as a surprise for her 35th birthday."

In reformulation, you may want to refocus, verify what matters most to the customer, and prioritize the different aspects that influence his choice:

"So what matters most for your wife is the originality and elegance of the handbag."

Reformulation shows you have listened.

Story 5

Checking into a five star hotel recently, the receptionist asked an interesting question of the guest checking in:

"Sir, would you please give me one or two things that we can do to make sure your stay is pleasurable and memorable?"

The guest was surprised to have this question asked at check-in. In the polite silence, he came up with a couple of things that would make his stay enjoyable.

For the outcome, see page 150.

Customers are cherry pickers of uniqueness and creativity. Their favorite book is called The Cherry on the Cake. *As a great storyteller, Sales Ambassadors build the cake layer by layer to showcase the cherry. Start the romance with a layer of mystery to excite their curiosity, a layer of sparkles to create their desire to own the cherry, and a layer of precious care to emphasize its value and uniqueness. Most important is for the Sales Ambassadors to work their magic and awaken the customer's emotional reasons for acquiring the cherry.*

—*Charlotte Duntze*
On-Premise Sales Manager,
Moët Hennessy, United States

Proposing, Romancing, and Handling Objections

Keep your proposals *simple*

59

The Sales Ambassador has listened and discovered what the customer is looking for. Now is the moment to make a proposal that responds to the request. The Sales Ambassador is careful not to confuse or overwhelm the customer with the proposal.

A consultant we know in London was seriously thinking of buying a luxury sports car. One morning, when he was walking to a meeting, a dealer's auto transport trailer went past him transporting six new models of the car he was interested in purchasing. He immediately lost his desire for the car. It no longer seemed special.

The same can happen to any sale. Putting out too many pieces also diminishes the uniqueness of each piece. Even if there are several examples or variations on the creations, the Sales Ambassador avoids bringing them all out together.

A proposal should consist of three or five options.

To keep your offer unique and valuable, keep it simple.

Create *curiosity*

60

Curiosity goes back to the love of surprises we had as children—being intrigued, wondering, and wanting to find out. By creating curiosity, the Sales Ambassador makes the exchange with the customer intriguing, interesting, and fun. Many approaches can make this happen:

"I wonder how the creation you are wearing would look with these shoes."

By stating it in this way, the customer wants more than to simply wonder. She wants to see and experience the ensemble.

In another situation with a customer, the Sales Ambassador brings out something that is quietly set to one side and not opened, while other pieces are shown. After a few moments, the customer wants to know what's in the box.

"This is an exceptional piece," the Sales Ambassador responds, and continues to ignore the box on the table. After a few more minutes, the customer is eager to see what is in the box. The Sales Ambassador, with a few more hesitations, opens the box. The delay has added magic and mystery to the piece and to the situation. A Sales Ambassador can also use the telephone to inform the customer that something wonderful has just arrived and that he is setting it aside for her:

"This morning, while opening the arrival of our new models, I noticed one particular creation which I have put aside for you. I feel quite sure that you will want to come in and see it."

The Sales Ambassador has created desire on the part of the customer to come in and experience the model first hand.

Remember the child within us all.

Handle everything you sell as a *precious* object

61

Scenario 1

On a mystery visit in New York for a luxury brand, we observed an Asian woman with her daughter shopping at the counter next to us. The women pointed to a handbag that was on the display just behind the Sales Associate, who turned around and with one hand, pulled the handbag off the shelf. It started to slip from her hand, so she grasped it tighter, making the handbag momentarily become deformed and lose its shape. She held it out to the customer, who was reluctant to take it but then seemed to do so out of politeness. After looking at the handbag and making a few comments to her daughter, she smiled, set the handbag on the counter, and left.

Scenario 2

We replay the tape. After seeing and verifying that the handbag was indeed what the customers were looking for, the Sales Ambassador puts on a pair of white gloves. She prepares a tray on the counter, in front of the two women. She then carefully and securely picks up the handbag with two hands and sets it gently down on the tray. There, she carefully opens it so the customers can appreciate the workmanship and also imagine what will be put inside.

Comparing the two scenarios, we can easily see that they are as different as night and day.

By awkwardly picking up the creation to be shown to the customer, the Sales Associate turned off the potential customer. In the first example, there was no hope for a sale. Her approach reduced rather than added value to the model. In the second scenario, the elegance and careful handling of the handbag enhanced the possibility of making a sale. In her treatment of the creation, the Sales Ambassador has emphasized its uniqueness and value.

The Sales Ambassador realizes how much creativity, time, and effort have gone into models before their arrival in the store. Each creation is handled and packaged carefully. Once the creation is in the hands of the Sales Ambassador, it should be treated as an *objet d'art.*

Elegance and respect for the creation enhance its value.

Position the offer

62

When a Sales Ambassador has enough information to make a proposal, what is presented should be based on what the customer has shared during the discussion, discovery, and observation. At the same time, it is an opportunity for the Sales Ambassador to extend the offer.

For example, let's look at a new car purchase. The customer indicates he is looking for a very basic model that will get him to and from work and that can be used on an occasional vacation trip. The Sales Ambassador asks if it would be all right to take the customer out for a test-drive in the model that is already in front of the showroom: *"Basically, it is the same car."*

The customer agrees, but is soon seduced by the extra options, the leather seats, air conditioning, and a slightly more powerful engine. After the test-drive, the model with fewer options that he was originally interested in seems far too dull.

Much of the success of extending the offer depends on the emotional aspect of a purchase. If some of the proposals are really beyond their budget, customers will convey this to Sales Ambassadors by their remarks and behavior. Going beyond the initial request is one of the most important skills Sales Ambassadors have.

In positioning the proposal, other aspects can come up by chance and can be used by the Sales Ambassador. For example, a couple looking at engagement rings have been very clear that their budget is limited. The Sales Ambassador brings out three rings, one in the price range they have indicated, and two of higher value.

In trying on one of the higher-value rings, the Sales Ambassador mentions that the carat is 2.28. The couple smile, sharing that they had first met on February 28. *"Then this is your ring!"* the Sales Ambassador added.

They bought the ring.

Extend every proposal.

Make clever use
of the *light*

63

Light is life; very few human beings live in the dark.
We need light for the creations and models we are selling.

What would a fashion show be without light?

What about photography without its flash?

How could a diamond show its brilliance and fire without light?

What would be the color of a red Bordeaux wine without light?

When showing models to customers, the Sales Ambassador always makes sure to take advantage of the light to enhance the beauty of each piece.

Verify the lighting in your windows and inside your boutique.

Light is a powerful ally in the process of seduction and attraction.

Romance your creations to *enhance* the emotions

64

Customers are buying more than just the functionality of the piece. For example, someone buying a luxury watch is looking for more than just a way to tell time. Customers are buying a dream. Sales Ambassadors know that by romancing the creation, they are reinforcing the desire to own the model being presented.

While factual information does have a role to play, it does not add anything to the emotional side of the sale:

"This ring has a diamond of 1.98 carat with a princess cut, an 'F' color, and VS2 clarity. It is a great investment."

Romance is all about raising the emotional interest and desire. It can be used to explain the symbolism of a creation:

"This precious diamond symbolizes the love that you found together. The exceptional quality gives a unique brilliance that you will enjoy every day."

This approach can be very effective when used with the customer's other motivations to purchase.

Create a link between the piece and the customer.

Storytelling

65

Storytelling is thousands of years old. Why do we enjoy hearing and listening to stories? Because they enlighten and entertain; they inform and educate; they pass on information and create the desire to learn more.

The Sales Ambassador develops the skills to be able to tell each story well. To hold the listener's attention, Sales Ambassadors think of ways to portray animation using their voice and body language. They know the impact this can have on customers who not only become more knowledgeable through this learning experience, but also find pleasure in the creation because of the story behind it.

Is there an association with a famous person and the model? If so, what happened that associates that person with the piece? What is the story behind the name of the creation? What about the choice of elements that make up the piece? What about the design itself? What inspired it and why is it unique?

A Sales Ambassador told the story behind a well-known cosmetic and how a certain movie star always used the product. The film star was one of the customer's favorites, and she was pleasantly surprised to learn that this actress swore by the product, and so she could not resist the desire to own it herself.

In another situation, the Sales Ambassador pointed out how the house had been designing dresses from celebrity weddings to designs worn at the Oscars in Hollywood.

In telling the story, the Sales Ambassador also gives customers something to share with others. Later, when they are showing the piece to someone else, they are able to pass on to others what they have learned.

Telling exciting and relevant stories about the creation makes it come to life.

Invite the customer to *try on* the model

66

A customer went to a clothing store out of curiosity, with no intention to buy. Noticing a beautiful jacket with no price tag, she asked a Sales Ambassador what the price was. Before even mentioning the price, the Sales Ambassador helped the lady try on the jacket. It was so wonderful and comfortable, she could not imagine leaving the boutique without it. But she not only bought the jacket. Caught up in the dream, she also purchased a matching skirt and a sweater.

Another customer was interested in buying a car. The Sales Ambassador let the customer take the car for a drive over to his house where he could pick up his wife and children for a quick spin. The car soon became a part of the customer's life.

What about wine? Tasting a good wine can lead someone to buy a case.

Experiences like these often lead to attachment. **Touching, smelling,** and **tasting** awaken customers' senses and then appeal to their emotions.

Sales Ambassadors know that having customers try on (try out or taste) what they are interested in makes the experience more realistic. The creation immediately begins to belong to the person, a reflection of their personality and lifestyle. There is a rapid attachment to a beautiful object.

Customers sometimes need polite encouragement to try something on. Sales Ambassadors quickly add, *"It does not cost a thing to try it on. Just for the pleasure."* A mirror on hand shows how the creation fits with the customer.

It is just like the French proverb which says *"To try is to adopt."*

The more customers try on, try out, or taste, the more likely they are to purchase.

"Wrap" the price as if it were a gift

67

As we said earlier, price is only one factor in a purchase. We need to consider the emotional reasons for buying, especially the many facets of life which are celebrated by *"gifting"* someone dear and important to us. By stating the price alone, the emotional atmosphere desired may be lost. A Sales Ambassador also knows that it is better for the customer to bring up the price.

Imagine the following situations. A customer has just asked how much it costs: *"The price is X dollars."*

When stated this way, often there is an uncomfortable silence, a doubt on the part of the customer. When stated on its own, all the attention is focused on the cost, instead of the other reasons purchases are made.

By wrapping the price, the benefits and the advantages of the offer are given. The price then becomes only one of the aspects:

"This limited-edition piece at a value of X dollars is already turning into a collector's item. It will be an exceptional addition for your private collection."

"This stunning ring, which comes with a certificate guaranteeing its quality, has a value of X dollars. It is a beautiful way to mark your 10th anniversary, and your wife will enjoy this ring for a lifetime."

By presenting the price in this way, the Sales Ambassador reinforces the personal interests the customer has in the purchase.

Present prices in their beautiful packages.

The art of exploring
"Let me think about it"

68

"Let me think about it" has many meanings, one of which might be that the buyer really wants to think about it. But behind the five words may also be:

"Convince me that this is what I should buy."

"You have not understood what I am really looking for."

"Show me something else."

"Do I really need this?"

Sales Ambassadors never accept *"Let me think about it"* at face value. They find out more about why the customer hesitates and respond accordingly. The minute the phrase comes out, they start preparing questions and statements:

"What further information would you like?"

"What makes you hesitate?"

"You will have tremendous pleasure using this!"

"What else would you like to see?"

This approach helps continue the discussion and give the sale another opportunity. But what if the customer still insists? The best way is to accept that they really would like to think about it. Sales Ambassadors also make requests to better understand the commitment of the customer:

"Would you like to make a deposit?"

"Shall I put this aside for you?"

When the customer departs, it is always on a positive note:

"Please feel free to return and I will be more than happy to help you. It was a pleasure to serve you today."

Remember that "Let me think about it" may not mean what it appears to mean.

Prepare for dealing with objections

59

Objections are perfectly normal. They are also opportunities to convince and persuade your customer that she is making good decisions.

Here are eight approaches that can be used together or separately:

1. Accept the customer's right to have an objection.
2. Listen without interrupting.
3. Ask questions to find out more about the objection.
4. Restate what you have understood.
5. Offer alternatives.
6. Reformulate to show that you have heard what has been said.
7. Go back over the benefits and use the discovery made earlier to point out why you feel this responds to their request.
8. Reassure the customer that this is a good solution.

Stay cool, structured, and positive when dealing with objections.

Story 6

The Sales Ambassador observed the woman carefully as she looked at herself in the mirror with a designer handbag over her shoulder. As she glanced at herself and the beautiful creation, she said *"Well, let me think about it."*

The Sales Ambassador watched the body language carefully and for the moment did not say anything. The woman did not take the bag off her shoulder; she did not put it back on the shelf. She continued to look into the mirror, while having the beautiful handbag.

For the outcome, see page 150.

Part Seven: Concluding and Making Additional Sales

*To conclude is the climax of the sale, but
also a phase where everything can fall apart.
The conclusion must be fluid and feel
natural, something that is perfectly normal
to the customer, without stopping the desire
created or expressed. To conclude a sale is
to make the dream or desire a reality, with
the proposal of the additional sale being as
natural as the conclusion.*

*The conclusion of a sale is simply a new
beginning. Just like the source of inspi-
ration specific to the luxury brands, the
process continues.*

*—Olivier Perruchot
General Manager,
Piaget France*

Be aware

of *buying signals*

70

A customer acts differently when she decides to purchase something, even if the three words *"I'll take it"* have not been said. Sales Ambassadors know that the decision first takes place in the mind of the customer and then in the expressed words. They pick up on the buying signals so that the conclusion is successful.

Body language and head movements differ according to what is going on in the customer's mind. Some clues may be a sparkle in the eyes and fewer questions. The model is held in the hand or worn, and the customer answers her own objections. Sometimes wanting information concerning the maintenance and guarantee, or an enquiry concerning payment, can be a signal.

Customers are not the same when it comes to concluding. Some appreciate a bit of silence to reflect. Others need more persuasion from the Sales Ambassador.

Some customers may feel that they have given a clear signal and expect the Sales Ambassador to pick up on it. If the Sales Ambassador misses the signal, the customer may interpret the delay as a negative and walk away.

Many Sales Associates have lost a sale right at the conclusion by failing to pick up on the buying signals. Some sales are also lost because the Sales Associate has failed to establish a person-to-person relationship and has failed to discover the real desire of the customer.

Watch and talk to Sales Ambassadors about concluding. Remember that customers are different. This remains true when it comes to concluding, in particular for some people when you are going to take their money.

Read the buying signals when concluding.

Tips to *Conclude*

71

To help conclude, Sales Ambassadors keep a certain number of additional details of the offer in reserve. These positive "surprises" make the customer even more pleased about the idea of purchasing. The offer becomes even more enticing with further personal additions.

A Sales Ambassador shared with us that when selling watches linked to a personal event, she first would say how pleased she was to participate in the event. She then would offer a personalized engraving on the watch for the customer. This approach was highly successful. Offering the engraving was also effective when selling two watches to a couple.

Sharing ways to offer positive and personalized surprises can also reinforce the emotional side of a purchase:

✦ Show the piece in its presentation case,

"Imagine her reaction when she opens this."

✦ Evoke the notion of ownership,

"This evening, think of the pleasure you will have wearing this!"

✦ Suggest gift wrapping,

"We would be more than happy to offer you a beautiful gift wrapping to surprise your daughter."

✦ Propose a home delivery,

"We would be pleased to deliver this to your home."

✦ Suggest complimentary services (alterations or exchanges),

"If for any reason you would like to exchange this, we will take care of it with pleasure."

Keep some positive surprises for the conclusion.

72

Suggest the best solution

Sales Ambassadors make suggestions to customers about what they are seeking. In the statement, the Sales Ambassador also suggests what is felt to be the best choice, based on the information given by the customer. This is particularly helpful when the customer is having trouble deciding:

"This creation responds to your wish to own something that will please now and for many years to come."

"You mentioned earlier how much you are a fan of our brand."

"This piece is unique. You mentioned that you were looking for something very creative and unusual."

Following these examples, the Sales Ambassador includes the customer in the discussion with a phrase such as *"What do you think?"*

These statements aim to win the customer's approval by linking her own personal opinions with the offer. This approach can play an important role in finalizing the purchase.

In concluding, advise the customer honestly on the best choice.

73 The importance of *reassuring* when concluding

In the mystery shoppings we have conducted, one of the phases that is often analyzed and evaluated is the conclusion. To carry out this phase, we actually make a purchase to see what is said and done. After discussion and a careful look at the models, we agree to make the purchase. We then listen to what is said next. Far too often, the first thing the Sales Associate says is: *"How would you like to pay?"*

What the Sales Associate has just said is that our relationship is based solely on the purchase. She is thinking short term and not building loyalty. Her words say: ***"You are a customer to me and no more."***

Some Sales Associates even lose sales at the conclusion. Although myriad reasons may cause this to happen, a typical one is the failure to make the customer feel good about having purchased. There is still a seed of doubt: ***"Maybe I should wait; maybe the one around the corner is nicer and I should go back and see it one more time; maybe I don't really need this now."***

These mental conversations are taking place, even though they just said, ***"I'll take it."***

It's still not too late for them to change their mind.

The Sales Ambassador realizes the fragility of this moment and takes her time. The phrase *"I'll take it"* (or one similar) triggers several sincere responses, even a reminder of what was discovered at the beginning of the contact:

"You have made a wonderful choice. You are going to enjoy this for many years to come; it is something that will give you years of pleasure. You mentioned that you wanted something for (travel, evening wear, everyday use). Well this is going to be perfect for that."

And all of those little conversations in the mind about waiting, going to see the one around the corner again, or simply not buying at all just melt away.

Reassuring the customer is key to concluding successfully.

74

"*Picture*" the purchase

Buying a precious gift is very special and is something that does not happen every day. The purchase of a gift has great positive emotional value.

Last January, we went to a restaurant to celebrate a friend's birthday. She was very pleased to see a special cake with her name written on it.

The restaurant staff went even further. They took photographs of the party and gave one to each person. Of course, we were very pleased that they had thought of doing this. We all took home a picture as a reminder of a wonderful evening together.

Capturing the moment is something many customers appreciate.

By "immortalizing" the purchase,
the Sales Ambassador gives the unexpected.

75

Advise customers about *maintaining* their purchase

From speaking with customers, we learned another interesting reason why they decided not to do business again with a brand. This has to do with not being informed about cleaning and taking care of a purchase, as the following true story shows.

A woman bought an expensive pair of boots from a reputable brand. At the time of purchase, the customer had a very positive experience with the Sales Associate.

The customer enjoyed wearing the new boots, but started to notice that certain areas were soon looking a little scuffed. Then one day she was caught out in the rain and her boots were left in bad shape. She then realized that the Sales Associate had not done her job. Suggestions and advice on how to care for her boots should have been given at the moment of purchase.

As this example points out, the woman would have bought the care product if it had been suggested, giving the Sales Associate an additional sale. Now the Sales Associate won't get the opportunity. She has lost a customer.

Why don't Sales Associates like talking about maintenance at the time of the purchase? The main reason given is that they fear losing a sale. What they forget is that even Rolls Royce owners know they have to change the oil, have the motor adjusted, and replace the tires.

When someone has bought an item needing a little special care and attention, Sales Ambassadors explain what needs to be done. They make suggestions about how purchases can be maintained and kept looking new for as long as possible. If maintenance and servicing are required in the future, the customer should be informed, so that there are no unexpected surprises.

To build loyalty, inform customers about taking care of their purchase.

Suggest ways
of *offering* a gift

76

"So tell me," the Sales Ambassador said as he finished the sale, *"When and how are you planning to give her this beautiful gift?"* The customer sat there with a blank stare for a moment, then said, *"I don't know."*

Often, people are concentrating more on what to buy than thinking about how they are going to present the gift. If the gift is for a special occasion, the time and manner of the presentation may be very important. The moment the gift is discovered is remembered for the rest of someone's life.

Suggestions from Sales Ambassadors are often appreciated. Once again, participation in the act of giving is more than just creative fun. The person giving the gift will also remember that the Sales Ambassador helped make the event even more exceptional.

Sales Ambassadors work with the customer to find the best and most surprising solution. Where could the giving of the gift take place? At what time should the gift appear? What would surprise the person receiving the gift the most?

A Sales Ambassador pointed out to a customer that taking the gift (a pair of earrings) with him to a restaurant would be difficult to hide and could spoil the surprise he wanted to have for his wife. The Sales Ambassador agreed to become an accomplice. That evening, at just the right moment, the Sales Ambassador came by the table with two glasses of champagne. The earrings were carefully placed in the bottom of the wife's glass.

Making the moment magic makes the gift even more stunning.

The *additional* sale

77

A customer has decided to make a purchase. The opportunity of proposing an additional sale presents itself. Some Sales Ambassadors are excellent at making the additional sale while others have enormous difficulty in doing so. What is the best approach?

The Sales Ambassador has various options, based on what has taken place:

✦ A couple, where the man has just purchased for the woman,

"Now, Sir, let's take a look at something for yourself!"

✦ A purchase of a handbag,

"I have just the shoes to go with it."

✦ A gift being bought for a friend,

"What would you like to see from our new collection?"

✦ A gift being bought for the new mother,

"We also have beautiful charms for babies."

The proposal for an additional sale should always make sense. It should avoid being a closed question (*"Anything else?"* loses every time).

When is the ideal time to propose the additional sale? Obviously, each situation varies somewhat. But most Sales Ambassadors feel the best time is after they have concluded the first sale.

It may be a situation where a customer promptly indicates that she does not wish to buy anything else, and it should be left at that.

Other times, a proposal is seen as a positive continuation of what she has just bought. A Sales Ambassador is sensitive to these issues, always proposing when appropriate.

Make the additional sale purchase part of the pleasure.

Story 7

The Sales Ambassador and the woman customer had spent several hours together in the luxury fashion boutique. The woman had just been promoted to an important position in her company, increasing her contacts with clients. Along with this, she would have many stand-up presentations to give at meetings and conferences in the near future. The Sales Ambassador also discovered that there would be a number of evening events. After trying on several outfits, the customer hesitated between three business/dress suits. All three were elegant and went well with the customer's taste and style. The exchanges and suggestions from the Sales Ambassador were both honest and helpful.

"Which one do you think I should choose?" the customer asked.

How do you think this concluded? See page 151.

In our hotel we frequently discuss the conversion of our first- or second-time visitors into "Customers for Life." We want to differentiate our service and personalized attention so much that customers will feel uncomfortable, or in the best case scenario, will be unable to defect to another hotel. Even if they do stay somewhere else, their experience will then begin to be consciously compared to the Four Seasons' experience.

—*Tracy Mercer*
General Manager,
Four Seasons Hotel Tokyo, Marunouchi

78

Loyalty comes from *offering* *gifts* linked to the purchase

Gifts are ways to thank customers for a purchase they have just made. The gesture shows that they are special to the Sales Ambassador and sincerely appreciated.

Once, a customer purchased a high-tech stereo system. He was very impressed by the Sales Ambassador who offered a maintenance kit and a special limited-edition CD of music with the purchase. When hearing a friend was looking for a similar solution, the customer immediately recommended the Sales Ambassador and his store.

Gifts increase each customer's pleasure. An extra watch strap, a travel pouch, a bottle of perfume, or a tie. . . . All leave a positive memory of the purchase.

Please your customers with gifts.

Offer *two* business cards

79

Business cards are one of your least expensive tools and one of your best resources for future business. They make contacting you easier.

Being generous, either at the point of interest or at the point of sale, increases your opportunity of extending your network. Whether the person buys or not, the cards end up in the handbags or wallets and into the worlds of the new people the Sales Ambassador has just met.

One for the person who came with the customer.

One for the office and one for home.

One for a friend who is looking for something similar.

One for the person receiving the gift (placed in the gift package).

Business cards also create another opportunity. Once the business cards have been given, it is much easier for the Sales Ambassador to ask for one of the customer's cards in return.

Double the chances; give two business cards each time.

Make a good
last impression

80

You hear a great deal of talk about the importance of a good first impression (and we have talked about it, too). The last impression is also important. Whether a customer has purchased or not, what Sales Ambassadors say and how they behave at the end of their contact leaves a lasting impression on the customer.

If this impression is positive and polite, the customer will want to return. If the customer is treated with indifference once the Sales Associate becomes aware that he is not going to buy; well, it is no surprise that the customer may be thinking, *"I might as well try somewhere else."*

A Sales Ambassador understands that the positive attention given to a customer should remain through the entire visit, whether the customer has purchased or not. Going to the door and opening it is really a minimum. In just a few seconds, you show an enormous respect for the customer. Some Ambassadors even go further, accompanying their customers to their cars, or when there is a purchase, offering to deliver it to the customer's house or hotel.

Last impressions are lasting impressions.

81 Every departure is a *preparation* for another visit

When the Sales Ambassador accompanies the customer to the door, her thoughts go back to what was said earlier while discovering the universe of her customer. More than just *"Goodbye, and thank you,"* the Sales Ambassador personalizes the departure, referring to specific aspects of the customer's visit. If she has bought a gift, the Sales Ambassador informs the customer that she hopes to see her again soon, to find something for herself.

Opportunities for positive exchanges with a customer abound in the moments just before leave-taking. When adding to the customer's file, note an up-and-coming important date or any special interests. At the door, remind her you would love to see her again. Propose that she give you a call at the number on the business card you have given her to let you know when she will be coming, so that you can block your time and be available. Or suggest giving her a call.

Something else very special is happening here. The Sales Ambassador is showing that she is not simply interested in the single purchase. She is also interested in keeping the contact and the relationship.

Sales Ambassadors take the time after a sale to make a few notes about their contact. This way, they can prepare pro-actively for future contacts with the customer. It is a good moment to plan a future contact by noting in their planner when and how they will recontact the customer.

There is a real desire to keep the relationship alive. As the customer leaves, there is always sincerity when the Sales Ambassador asks, *"When will I see you again?"*

Think beyond the sale. Start thinking and setting up customers for life.

Loyalty comes from
remembering your customers

82

The Sales Ambassador glances up as the customer walks into the store. He recognizes the customer and goes toward him:

"Mr. Wong, how nice to see you again! How did Ms Wong like the gift you bought her, what was it, three months ago? And is your daughter back from university?"

Mr. Wong is more than impressed. He realizes that something stronger than the customer-sales associate contact has been established. It goes beyond the Sales Ambassador giving him VIP treatment. It is a person-to-person contact.

Memory is a key aspect in a Sales Ambassador's success. Remembering shows the customer that he matters as a person. From one short visit, the two of you have established a relationship that goes beyond the making of a purchase.

Remembering shows that the customer matters.

The *database* is an essential *tool*

83

It is impossible to remember everything about every customer. So to be effective, Sales Ambassadors review their customer database to update and review the information they have compiled.

First of all, the database improves the quality and efficiency of the sale. By knowing what the customer has already purchased (or owns), a Sales Ambassador can make better proposals. Using the data, a more personalized service adapted to the preferences of the customer can be provided.

The database also builds and reinforces loyalty. Along with the name and contact information, the Sales Ambassador completes the information with what has come up during exchanges and conversation with the customer. Criteria such as family, interests, important dates, events, lifestyle, profession, and the customer's network of personal contacts are some of the main categories. Often, Sales Ambassadors add comments such as *"Mr. Wong prefers coffee to tea." "Ms Klein owns horses."*

Spend time with your database every day.

Celebrate the newborn

84

Nothing is more emotional than the birth of a child. A new addition is adored by family and friends, and where the baby does not travel, the photos certainly do. The excitement and joy of this moment are a celebration of life itself.

Sales Ambassadors participate in this unique event by congratulating and verifying that everyone is doing well (even the father, who can find the process very stressful). A card with a gesture of flowers or something else appropriate is sent, always in a very personalized way.

There are other ways of marking this special event. One of the possibilities is an engraving on a specific piece for the child. Putting the child's name and birth date on a beautiful creation is something they will keep for a lifetime.

When a Sales Ambassador does not sell anything appropriate for a new baby, one of the solutions is to go out and purchase something and have it engraved. In most cases, the newborn's parents take the time to come by and thank the Sales Ambassador. When they do, it is an excellent opportunity to share with them what is new in the boutique.

The newborn is not the only one deserving praise and attention. The baby's arrival is also an opportunity for the husband to offer a gift to his wife or for the couple to mark the event. Once again, the Sales Ambassador's role is to propose and participate in the event.

Of course the information and details about the new baby are put into the customer file and brought up when appropriate in the future.

Follow up on births among your customers and participate in the celebration.

Build loyalty

85 by *staying in touch*

You have not seen one of your customers in a while. The travel handbag that just came in is in one of your customer's favorite colors. There is a concert nearby featuring a favorite singer of a couple who shop regularly.

What are all of these, but a mixture of events and personal happenings that come into all of our lives at one time or another? For a Sales Ambassador, they are examples of situations where there is a good reason to contact customers.

There are a hundred reasons to recontact customers. Basically they fall into three categories: the purchase, the customer's personal events, and events around the universe of the brand.

The purchase
+ A note to thank the customer
+ In the case of a gift, to find out if the person who received it was pleased
+ To verify if the item purchased is working properly
+ In some situations, a reminder concerning servicing and maintenance to keep the warranty.

A customer's personal events
+ The wife's birthday is in two weeks
+ An interview in a local newspaper about one of your customers
+ Congratulations for a daughter's graduation

Events around the brand
+ An invitation to a special event (an art exhibition sponsored by the brand, an opening, a charity event)
+ The launching of a new collection
+ A new catalog

Special days

+ New Year's Day
+ Valentine's Day
+ Mother and Father's Day
+ National and religious days

It is essential to obtain the approval from the customer to be recontacted in the future. A proposal by the Sales Ambassador first explains the reasons why she wishes to contact the customer:

"This is our quarterly magazine that I would like to offer to you today. If you would like to receive it in the future, I would be more than happy to send it to you. May I take down your address? Would you like to receive our new catalog when it comes out? We would also like to invite you to our annual cocktail party."

How should customers be contacted? The customer and the Sales Ambassador should always make this decision. Some customers prefer the telephone, and others like to receive e-mails. Some prefer that all messages go to the office, others to the home.

How often should customers be contacted? If you have not seen someone in three to five months, it is a good idea to get in touch. Even a simple and sincere note of a few handwritten lines is always nice to receive. Remember that good quality paper, nice colored ink, and an interesting stamp make the letter more attractive.

Find good excuses to stay in touch.

Ask for a *referral*

86

As we have said earlier, there are customers behind customers. Each person can bring you something. Sometimes a sale or contact with an existing customer can bring you in contact with another person who might be a potential customer.

By requesting, the Sales Ambassador is increasing his network rapidly and at the same time creating opportunities for new customers. This approach requires a little time and can be used to quickly expand your network.

Think of the number of people we know, both professionally and personally. Some professions like doctors or dentists have hundreds of contacts.

Sales Ambassadors know whom to approach and how. A good relationship is necessary, regardless of whether there is a purchase. A customer who likes the brand is also likely to share his network and give you names of people interested in your services and creations.

Timing is of the essence. A few examples are:

+ After having offered a service,

"We are pleased to have helped you so quickly. I have a special request. Do you know someone I could contact about our service?"

◆ On the occasion of a new launching,

"We are organizing a cocktail party for the new collection and I am sending you an invitation. Is there someone else you would like me to invite?"

◆ After having found a solution for a contact,

"I know you are going to enjoy the restaurant tonight. It was a pleasure to use my contacts to book you a table. By the way, we just received some new catalogs. Is there someone you would like me to send one to?"

Follow-up to referrals is also important. When the new contacts do come by, Sales Ambassadors make sure they inform and thank their initial source.

Use referrals to value contacts and grow your business.

Customer after-sales service
87 and the *broken dream*

Mary's beautiful watch has stopped running. This wonderful gift was from her parents when she graduated from university four years ago, and she has worn it every day. Mary knows where they bought it because she has been back several times for new straps.

The fact that it is not working is a nuisance to her because it is the only watch she owns. It has an automatic movement, so she knows it's not going to be a simple battery change. She now has to take it in for servicing and quickly find an alternative so that she can know the time.

There is also something that goes beyond the simple service. Mary never dreamed of owning such a precious object. So she brings back a broken dream into the boutique.

A thoughtful Sales Ambassador understands and anticipates the double frustration someone often feels when bringing in an object needing servicing. It is much more than simply taking down the serial number, filling in the after-sales service form, and telling the customer she will be contacted when the estimate is made.

Each service visit is an opportunity to create or update a customer file. It is a possibility to suggest or propose an alternative (perhaps Mary could consider purchasing another watch to wear on different occasions). The Sales Ambassador can also use the visit to create desire for other purchases. Knowing that she'll be coming back eventually to pick up her watch, it would be interesting to give her a catalog and some options to think about.

Boutiques could also offer a consignment watch for the maintenance period. That way, two of Mary's problems are taken care of in one visit: her watch will come back like new, and she will not be showing up late for her appointments.

Look at every after-sales service visit as an opportunity.

The *ideal* after-sales service scenario

88

Brands spend millions in publicity to attract and get people to come into their boutiques. Yet everyday, customers come in without the appeal of advertising. They are back with a problem. Something they purchased or received as a gift is not working or needs servicing.

The Sales Ambassador sees after-sales service as an opportunity. She understands the situation, finds a solution, establishes (or reestablishes) contact, and prepares to see the customer again.

The customer who needs after-sales service is always greeted warmly and is as welcome as any other customer. To gain valuable information about the object that needs servicing, the Sales Ambassador begins with open questions and active listening. The questions also let the customer express the emotional part of his frustrations.

There is ownership of the problem: *"Here's what I can do for you"* from the Sales Ambassador, with a clear commitment as to when the piece will be ready.

To give added value to the servicing, the Sales Ambassador communicates the details of what will be done during the intervention together with the amount. She also validates that the customer is in agreement.

The contact is also a good moment to obtain and update information on the customer for recontacting him to communicate the estimate or to inform him when the service is completed.

During the servicing period, if the Sales Ambassador has new or more specific information, a telephone call is made to the customer to give an update.

When the customer returns, the Sales Ambassador reviews the service and makes sure any use and care advice are clearly communicated. The return visit is also the moment to propose new items, offer a catalog, and give information on upcoming launches and events.

Make every after-sales service visit impeccable.

Story 8

One of the ways a Sales Ambassador prepares is to reflect on which customers are going to be contacted. Two questions the Sales Ambassador asks are, "Who haven't I seen in a while?" and "Who could I contact concerning a specific creation that has come in or an event that is going on?"

One boutique manager we know requires that every day, each of her eight Sales Ambassadors write two brief letters to two of their customers that they have not seen in a while. The letters could be just a few lines from the Sales Ambassador, but it has to be personalized, which requires the Sales Ambassadors to look at the customer files to refresh their memory concerning purchases and preferences.

The boutique purchased very elegant stationery and envelopes as well as collector stamps to be used for the letters. Before leaving, each of the Sales Ambassadors had to put the two letters he had written on the Manager's desk.

For the impact, see page 151.

Outcomes of the Eight Stories

Story 1

Our VIP customer hung up and decided to write checks to his friends who had been obliged to pay for their parking. It was not the cost, but it was simply unacceptable that they had to pay for coming to his dinner party. He then started to look around for other places to spend his money when he wanted to stay someplace nice.

By charging for parking and the way he was treated, the luxury hotel lost a client and a considerable amount of revenue.

Story 2

In the end, the customer left with a free watch strap . . . and an elegant beautiful new platinum timepiece to add to his collection.

Story 3

The customer decided he wanted to take the creation, but because of his condition, could not come and pick up the purchase. When the Sales Ambassador offered to deliver it personally, the sale was made.

Story 4

This customer was very touched and has remained loyal over the years, purchasing several cases of champagne annually. It is interesting to note that a little attention to detail, to something very personal, can go a long way.

Story 5

The requests brought up at the moment of checking in were taken care of impeccably by the staff during the guest's stay. The customer also noticed that many other aspects were improved. In fact, the guest was benefiting from other customers having answered the same question at check-in.

Four months later the guest came back for a five-night stay.

Story 6

Often (and this situation is a perfect example), when the item in question is kept in the intimate space of the potential buyer (they continue to wear it), and he or she states *"Let me think about it,"* it means something entirely different. The body language is saying what the person is really feeling. Most likely, the person wants to be convinced that she should purchase the creation.

In this case, the Sales Ambassador went back to discovery, remarked how the designer bag was the favorite color of the would-be buyer and would be perfect for daily wear. Even though the Sales Ambassador was told one thing, she "listened" to the body language, and made the sale.

This is not only applicable with handbags. It is true with nearly all purchases. Someone who still has a watch on and says he wants to think about it is saying the same thing as the lady with the handbag still on her shoulder. Someone who continues to sit in the car he has just test-driven and states that he needs to think about it is also indicating that he wants to be convinced.

Story 7

The Sales Ambassador spoke with sincerity:

"If I were you, I'd take all three. You're going to be seeing the same customers on more than one occasion, and one or two of the outfits might be at the cleaners. So the other one is available. But what is most important is that you look great in all of them!"

She bought all three.

Story 8

When starting this, the manager admitted that there was resistance. How were they going to squeeze in one more thing in a very busy day? But like everything else, once it started rolling, it became easier and faster, and the investment was well worth it.

There was a measurable increase in the number of customers that called in, came by, and purchased. The math is also interesting. Assuming a five-day week, eight Sales Ambassadors, two letters a day, multiplied by 52 weeks, you come up with over 4,000 personalized customer contacts yearly for the boutique! From this, the CRM of the company followed up, noting that 16 percent (over 640) of those contacted came by the boutique, with 250 people making purchases. Another positive outcome was that a lot of "sleeping customers" became active again.

Conclusion

"There is no greater gift that a Sales Ambassador can receive than praise from a customer. I would like to share the following excerpt from a letter sent to us, after a considerable purchase was made by a couple. It says it all:

'We both are still impressed by our experience and would like to thank you for your outstanding service. Your professionalism as well as your obvious dedication and passion for your work is simply inspiring . . . . I think it was so far the greatest buy in my life. For sure the value of this one of a kind experience equals at least the value of the stone. We feel honored to have had the opportunity to share it with you and will treasure it deep inside our hearts. One of the diamond's many facets will surely remind us of you for a lifetime. Thank you so much for everything you did for us.'"

Hamida Belkadi, CEO
DeBeers Diamond Jewelers, USA

Opportunities present themselves every day for Sales Ambassadors to learn and become better at what they do. Pleasure comes from going even further and capitalizing on the skills and abilities already acquired. With constant new challenges for building relationships, each sales situation offers unique differences with new possibilities for growing and expanding our knowledge.

Aristotle said *"We are what we continuously do. Therefore excellence is not an act; it is a habit."* Achieving excellence then is all about developing good habits. This requires the ability to learn new approaches and practice them regularly.

We are sure that by now you have understood that Sales Ambassadors have an important role to play for the brand. After all that is done upstream, it is their turn to bring in the sale. Selling is a complex art and requires a quick mind that observes and understands human behavior. We have said it before, but it is worth repeating: the Sales Ambassadors who succeed are those who build trust from the very first contact with their customers.

Some of *Selling Luxury* has certainly been a confirmation of what you were already using in your contacts with customers. Other ideas bring you new ways of creating the experience to **astonish customers every time.**

Sales Ambassadors learn through observing how other people approach customer service. If they are open-minded, they can pick up ideas from a variety of different contacts, from waiters and airline hostesses to people selling in supermarkets and lecturers in museums. Sales Ambassadors also share ideas about their excellent customer service experiences with colleagues and managers.

We suggest that you fine-tune your approach to selling by concentrating on improving one or two key skills at a time.

The "sharpening" of your skills is something Sales Ambassadors continuously work on throughout their careers. Building your abilities is, at the same time, a fun and enriching experience.

So how can you keep going? There's work to be done to assimilate and grow personally. To begin with, **assume you have room for improvement.**

Stay in shape.

Index

Active listening, 84
Additional sales, ways to make, 126–127
After-sale service:
    broken dreams and, 144–145
    ideal scenario for, 146–147
Alternative purchases, timing and, 41
Apologies, offering during busy times, 66, 67
Appointments, suggesting at busy times, 67
Aristotle, 153
Assistance, providing to other team members, 53
Atmosphere, importance of store's, 63–64

Belkadi, Hamida, 153
Births, celebrating of, 138–139
Body language:
    buying signals and, 115–116
    when welcoming customers, 76
Bousseffa, Eric, 73
Brand:
    care and maintenance advice about, 123–124
    discovering how customer feels about, 85
    handling objects with elegance and respect, 98–99
    sale ambassador as, 3–5
    staying in touch with events around, 140
    thanking customer for choosing, 81
Broken dreams, after-sales service and, 144–145
Business cards:
    exchanging of, 87
    offering two, 132
Busy times:
    helping customers during, 51–52
    keeping service level up during, 66–67
Buying signals, being aware of, 115–116

Care, giving advice about purchase, 123–124
Cartier, 1, 17
Catalog, offering to send, 55
Celebrations, reminding customers of occasions for, 38
Celine, 35
Choice:
    advising honestly on best, 119
    customer's other choices as competition, 11
    timing and, 40
Christian Dior, 61
City, providing information about, 71
Clothing, getting clues about customers from, 77–78
Competition:
    customer's other choices as, 11
    knowing about, 48
    learning what customer thinks about, 85
    seeing "not buying" as, 26–27
Complaints, seeing as opportunity, 25

Complimentary services, offering of, 118
Compliments, offering to customer, 24
Concluding of sale, 113
    advising on care and maintenance, 123–124
    buying signals and, 115–116
    "immortalizing" purchase, 122
    reassuring and, 120–121
    staying in touch after, 140
    story and outcome, 128, 151
    suggesting best solution, 119
    suggesting ways to give, 125
    timing and, 41
    tips for, 117–118
Confidentiality, importance of, 14
Congratulations, offering to customer, 23
Consistency, importance of, 50
Contacts, turning into experiences, 20
Creations. *See* Brand
Curiosity, creating in customer, 96–97
Customers. *See also* Emotions; Welcoming and discovering
    acquiring for life, 134–135
    adapting to needs of, 56–57
    consulting with about ways to stay in touch, 141
    cost of lost, 9
    listening to story of, 21–22
    providing enjoyable experience to, 8

Database, of customer information, 137
De Beers, 153
Details, paying attention to store's, 65
Discretion, importance of, 14
Display models, limiting of, 95
Doorman, hiring for busy times, 67
Duntze, Charlotte, 93

Emotions, of customer, 93
    creating curiosity, 96–97
    creating link between customer and piece, 103
    encouraging customer to try on piece, 106–107
    handling "Let me think about it" customer, 109–110
    handling objections, 111
    handling pieces with elegance and respect, 98–99
    keeping proposals simple, 95
    personalized surprises and, 117–118
    positioning proposal, 100–101
    presenting price, 108
    sale ambassador's role and understanding of, 10
    story and outcome, 112, 150
    telling stories, 104–105
    using light, 102
Energy, maintaining when busy, 51–52

Engraving, offering of, 117
Events and activities, of local area, 71
Expectations, exceeding of customer's, 13
Eyes, "listening" with, 77–78

Four Seasons, 129
Frame of mind, of Sales Ambassador, 17
    avoiding preconceived ideas and prejudices, 29
    complimenting customers, 24
    congratulating customers, 23
    establishing person-to-person contact, 19
    handling complaints, 25
    handling mistakes, 31–32
    listening to customer's story, 21–22
    making service gestures, 28
    seeing "not buying" as option, 26–27
    story and outcome, 33, 149
    turning contacts into experiences, 20
    working as team player, 30

Gift purchases, 81, 125
Gifts, with purchase, 131
Gift wrapping, offering of, 118
Guten, Michel, 1

Home delivery, offering of, 118

Impressions:
    importance of first, 6
    importance of last, 133
Introduction, of self, 87

"Just looking" customers, 88–89

Knowledge and information:
    about making of pieces, 70
    sharing with customer, 39

Lahirle, Jean, 35
Last impression, importance of good, 133
"Let me think about it" customers, 109–110
Le Troquer, François, 17
Lexus, 73
Light, using to advantage, 102
Listening skills:
    listening carefully, 84
    listening with eyes, 77–78
Lost sales, analyzing of, 58
Loyalty, building customer's, 129
    after-sales service and, 144–147
    asking for referrals, 142–143
    celebrating births, 138–139
    making good first impression, 6
    making good last impression, 133

offering gifts linked to purchase, 131
offering two business cards, 132
preparing for another visit, 134–135
product care advice and, 123–124
quality and service and, 7
remembering each customer, 136–137
staying in touch, 140–141
story and outcome, 148, 151

Maintenance, giving advice about product's, 123–124
Mental fatigue, handling of, 51
Mercer, Tracy, 129
Mistakes, handling of, 31–32
Moët Hennessy, 93
Music, as metaphor for selling, 45

Network, of customer, 8–9
Nicolas, Laurence, 61

Open questions, 79–80, 82–83
Open statements, 86
Organization, importance of, 68

Perrin, Alain Dominique, xi
Perruchot, Olivier, 113
Personal events, as reason to stay in touch, 138–139
Personalization, of service, 49
Person-to-person contact, establishing with
        customer, 19, 21–22
Photographs, providing of purchase, 122
Piaget, 113
Pieces. *See* Brand
Preconceived ideas, avoiding, 29
Prejudices, avoiding, 29
Preparation for selling, 61
    attending to details, 65
    creating atmosphere, 63–64
    knowing near-by events and activities, 71
    knowing stock, 69
    learning about creation of pieces, 70
    preparing selling tools, 68
    serving at busy times, 66–67
    story and outcome, 72, 149
Price:
    how to present, 108
    personalized service as justification of, 12
Proposals:
    keeping simple, 95
    positioning of, 100–101
    reformulating of, 90

Questions, asking open, 79–80,
Questions, quality over quantity, 82–83

Reassurance, at conclusion of sale, 120–121
Referrals, asking for, 142–143
Reformulation, of proposal, 90
Remembering, of customers:
    database for information, 137
    importance of, 136
Repeat business, 37
Romance, enhancing pieces with, 103

Sales:
    analyzing lost, 58
    analyzing successful, 56–57
Sales ambassadors, 1. *See also* Frame of mind;
        Savoir faire
    as the brand, 5
    choice and competition and, 11
    cost of lost customer and, 9
    customer treatment and, 7
    discretion/confidentiality and, 14
    emotions of purchase and, 10
    exceeding of expectations, 13
    experience of customer and, 8
    loyalty and trust in, 6
    price and, 12
    story and outcome, 15, 149
    vital role of, 3-4
Savoir-faire, of Sales Ambassador, 35
    analyzing lost sales, 58
    analyzing purchases, 56–57
    anticipating celebrations, 38
    being consistent, 50
    developing pleasant voice, 47
    giving time, 42–43
    helping others, 53
    knowing competition, 48
    maintaining energy, 51–52
    personalizing service, 49
    practicing/preparing/improvising, 45
    selecting words with care, 46
    selling style, 37
    sharing information, 39
    story and outcome, 59, 149
    timing comments and questions, 40–41
    using silence, 40, 44
    using telephone, 54–55
Selling style:
    definition of successful, 37
    having adaptable, 7, 77
Senses, appealing to customer's, 106–107
Services, offering to customer, 28
Silence, importance of occasional, 40, 44
Skills, sharpening of, 154

Smell, appealing to customer's sense of,
        106–107
Smiles:
    welcoming customers with, 75
    when speaking, 47
Special days, as reason to stay in touch, 141
Stock, knowing about available, 69
Storytelling, to make creation come to life,
        104–105
Surprises, to help conclude sale, 117–118

Taste, appealing to customer's sense of,
        106–107
Team/team work:
    during busy times, 51–52
    communication and, 30
    offering assistance, 53
Telephone contacts, tips for, 54–55
Time:
    power of proper timing, 40–41
    as sales tools, 42–43
Tools, preparing of selling, 68
Touch, appealing to customer's sense of,
        106–107
Trust, building with first contact, 6
Trying on, encouraging of, 106–107

Value, adding to purchase:
    with knowledge of competition, 48
    with respect for object, 98–99
Voice:
    improving tone and quality of, 47
    on telephone, 54

Welcoming and discovering, of customers, 73
    asking open questions, 79–80, 82–83
    greeting with smile, 75
    handling gift purchases, 81
    handling "just looking" customers, 88–89
    introducing self, 87
    learning customer's feelings about brand, 85
    listening and, 77–78, 84
    making open statements, 86
    reformulating proposal, 90
    story and outcome, 91, 150
    using body language well, 76
Words, choosing with care, 46
"Wow" experience, providing of, 13

Yearly events:
    as reason to stay in touch, 141
    reminding customers to celebrate, 38